D0056681

the purity myth

How America's
Obsession with
Virginity Is Hurting
Young Women

JESSICA VALENTI
Author of *Full Frontal Feminism*

PRAISE FOR JESSICA VALENTI

"A gutsy young third-wave feminist."
—LIESL SCHILLINGER, *The New York Times*

"Valenti's writing has a wonderful defiant quality reminiscent of
the days of the movement's youth."
—LINDA HIRSHMAN, *The Washington Post*

"It's hard not to love Jessica Valenti. The Brooklyn-based founder
of Feministing.com—the uncompromising, balls-out, feminist
blog—is brilliant, beautiful, and not even 30 years old."
—*BUST* *magazine*

"Fierce and funny. . . . In-your-face feminism is what Valenti
is about."
—ANTONIA ZERBISIAS, *The Toronto Star*

"[Feministing] it is head and shoulders above almost any writing
on women's issues in mainstream media."
—ALISSA QUART, *Columbia Journalism Review*

FOR *FULL FRONTAL FEMINISM*

"Valenti writes slangy, profane and disconcertingly funny prose.
 She's like the Fran Lebowitz of women's rights..."
—REBECCA TRAISTER, Salon.com

"Valenti's analysis is cogent and sharp."
—EMMA KIVISILD, *Herizons*

"...an irreverent guide to why young women should embrace
 the F-word."
—EMMA PEARSE, *New York Magazine*

"Valenti's book, packed with sound advice and solid research, is filled
 with enough wit and sass to convince young women that feminism
 is far from boring—that it is, in fact, necessary."
—PATRICIA JUSTINE TUMANG, *The Women's Review of Books*

The Purity Myth
How America's Obsession with Virginity Is Hurting Young Women

Copyright © 2009 by Jessica Valenti

Published by
Seal Press
A Member of Perseus Books Group
1700 Fourth Street
Berkeley, California

All rights reserved. No part of this book may be reproduced or transmitted in any form without written permission from the publisher, except by reviewers who may quote brief excerpts in connection with a review.

Library of Congress Cataloging-in-Publication Data

Valenti, Jessica.
 The purity myth : how America's obsession with virginity is hurting young women / Jessica Valenti.
    p. cm.
 ISBN-13: 978-1-58005-253-5
 ISBN-10: 1-58005-253-3
 1. Young women—Sexual behavior—United States. 2. Virginity—Social aspects—United States. I. Title.
 HQ29.V338 2009
 306.73—dc22
                        2008042226

Cover and Interior design by Domini Dragoone
Printed in the United States of America by Maple-Vail
Distributed by Publishers Group West

FOR ANDREW

contents

"I believe that there is an ideal of fastidiousness in the world. An ideal of impossible purity in a world that is, in its very essence, impure."

MARY GORDON
in *I Need to Tell Three Stories and to Speak of Love and Death*

introduction

THERE IS A MORAL PANIC IN AMERICA over young women's sexuality—and it's entirely misplaced. Girls "going wild" aren't damaging a generation of women, the myth of sexual purity is. The lie of virginity—the idea that such a thing even exists—is ensuring that young women's perception of themselves is inextricable from their bodies, and that their ability to be moral actors is absolutely dependent on their sexuality. It's time to teach our daughters that their ability to be good people depends on their *being good people*, not on whether or not they're sexually active.

A combination of forces—our media- and society-driven virginity fetish, an increase in abstinence-only education, and the strategic political rollback of women's rights among the primary culprits—has created a juggernaut of unrealistic sexual expectations for young women. Unable to live up to the ideal of purity that's forced upon them in one aspect of their lives, many young women are choosing the hypersexualized alternative that's offered to them everywhere else as the easier—and more attractive—option.

More than 1,400 purity balls, where young girls pledge their virginity to their fathers at a promlike event, were held in 2006 (the balls are federally funded).[1] Facebook is peppered with purity groups that exist to support girls trying to "save it." Schools hold abstinence rallies and assemblies featuring hip-hop dancers and comedians alongside religious leaders. Virginity and chastity are reemerging as a trend in pop culture, in our schools, in the media, and even in legislation. So while young women are subject to overt sexual messages every day, they're simultaneously being taught—by the people who are supposed to care for their personal and moral development, no less—that their only real worth is their virginity and ability to remain "pure."

So what are young women left with? Abstinence-only education during the day and Girls Gone Wild commercials at night! Whether it's delivered through a virginity pledge or by a barely dressed tween pop singer writhing across the television screen, the message is the same: A woman's worth lies in her ability—or her refusal—to be sexual. And we're teaching American girls that, one way or another, their bodies and their sexuality are what make them valuable. The sexual double standard is alive and well, and it's irrevocably damaging young women.

The Purity Myth is something I've been thinking about for a long time. When I lost my virginity as a high school freshman, I didn't understand why I didn't feel changed somehow. Wasn't this supposed to be, like, a big deal? Later, in college, as I'd listen to male friends deride their sexual partners as sluts and whores, I struggled to comprehend how intercourse could mean one thing for men and quite another for women. I knew that *logically,* nothing about sex could make a girl "dirty," but I found it incredibly frustrating that my certainty about this seemed to be lost on my male peers. And as I talked to my queer friends, whose sexual experiences were often dismissed because they didn't fit into the heterosexual model, I started to realize how useless "virginity" really was.

I started to see the myth of sexual purity everywhere—though in the work I do as a feminist blogger and writer, it wasn't exactly hard to find. Whether it appears in a story about a man killing his girlfriend while calling her a whore or in trying to battle conservative claims that emergency contraception or the HPV vaccine will make girls promiscuous, the purity myth in America underlies more misogyny than most people would like to admit.

And while the definition of "virginity" is fairly abstract (as you'll see in Chapter 1), its consequences for young women are not. And that's why I wanted, and needed, to write this book. *The Purity Myth* is for women who are suffering every day because of the lie that virginity exists, and that it has some bearing on who we are and how good we are. Consider the implications virginity has on the high school girl who is cruelly labeled a slut after an innocuous makeout session; the woman from a background so religiously conservative that she opts to have her hymen surgically reattached rather than suffer the consequences of a nonbloody bedsheet on her wedding night; or the rape survivor who's dismissed or even faulted because she dared to have past consensual sexual encounters.

My reasons for wanting to write this book aren't entirely altruistic, however. I was once that teenage girl struggling with the meaning behind my sexuality, and how my own virginity, or lack thereof, reflected whether or not I was a good person. I was the cruelly labeled slut, the burgeoning feminist who knew that something was wrong with a world that could peg me as a bad person for sleeping with a high school boyfriend while ignoring my good heart, sense of humor, and intelligence. Didn't the intricacies of my character count for anything? The answer, unfortunately, was no, they didn't. It was a hard lesson to learn, and one that too many young women are dealing with nationwide.

UNDERSTANDING THE MYTH

On Love Matters, a pro-life, pro-abstinence website, pictures of smiling young women who are "saving themselves" are featured next to quotes about virginity and marriage. Kimberly Gloudemans, Miss California Teen USA 1997, beams under her brunette coiffed hair and a rhinestone tiara. Next to her picture, the caption reads, "It's been echoed to teens over and over again . . . we have no morals, no dreams, and no future. But I know I am not a part of that same generation. In fact, millions of teenagers are finding out the same thing about themselves. . . . We have morals and are standing up for what we believe in. . . . Because of that I am saving sex for marriage."

I've always found the idea of "saving" your virginity intriguing: It's not as if we're packing our Saran-wrapped hymens away in the freezer, after all, or pasting them in scrapbooks (admittedly, not the best visual—my apologies). But packed-away virginities aside, the interesting—and dangerous—idea at play here is that of "morality." When young women are taught about morality, there's not often talk of compassion, kindness, courage, or integrity. There is, however, a lot of talk about hymens (though the preferred words are undoubtedly more refined—think "virginity" and "chastity"): if we have them, when we'll lose them, and under what circumstances we'll be rid of them.

While boys are taught that the things that make them men—good men—are universally accepted ethical ideals, women are led to believe that our moral compass lies somewhere between our legs. Literally. Whether it's the determining factor in our "cleanliness" and "purity" or the marker of our character, virginity has an increasingly dangerous hold over young women. It affects not only our ability to see ourselves as ethical actors outside of our own bodies, but also how the world interacts with us through social mores, laws, and even violence.

PURE CONSEQUENCES

Women are pushing themselves and punishing themselves every day in order to fit into the narrow model of morality that virginity has afforded them. Some of us get unnecessary plastic surgery—down to our vaginas, which can be tightened, clipped, and "revirginized"—in order to seem younger. Others simply buy into old-school gender norms of ownership, dependence, and perpetual girlhood.

And don't be mistaken about the underlying motivations of our moral panic around the hypersexualization of young women. It's more about chastity than about promiscuity. T-shirts sold in teen catalogs with I'M TIGHT LIKE SPANDEX emblazoned across the front aren't announcing sexiness; they're announcing virginity. The same is true for "sexy schoolgirl" costumes or provocative pictures of Disney teen pop singers. By fetishizing youth and virginity, we're supporting a disturbing message: that really sexy women aren't women at all—they're girls.

If we're to truly understand the purity myth, we have to recognize that this modernized virgin/whore dichotomy is not only leading young women to damage themselves by internalizing the double standard, but also contributing to a social and political climate that is increasingly antagonistic to women and our rights.

Virginity fetishism has even made its way into politics and legislation. In 2007, Republican South Dakota representative Bill Napoli described his support for a ban on abortion that allowed no exceptions for rape or incest by relaying a (quite vivid) scenario to a reporter. He explained under what circumstances the procedure *might* be warranted: "A real-life description to me would be a rape victim, brutally raped, savaged. The girl was a virgin. She was religious. She planned on saving her virginity until she was married. She was brutalized and raped, sodomized as bad as you can possibly make it, and is impregnated."[2]

I found this moment so telling: Napoli couldn't help but let his misogyny and paternalism seep into his abortion sound bite, because, to him and to so many other men (and other legislators, for that matter), there's no separating virginity, violence, and control over women's bodies. When it comes to women who are perceived as "impure," there's a narrative of punishment that underscores U.S. policy and public discourse—be it legislation that limits reproductive rights through the assumption that women should be chaste before marriage, or a media that demonizes victims of sexual violence. And, sadly, if you look at everything from our laws to our newspapers, Napoli isn't as far out of the mainstream as we'd like to think.

TOWARD A NEW MORALITY

Women—especially young women, who are the most targeted in this virgin/whore straitjacket—are surviving the purity myth every day. And it has to stop. Our daughters deserve a model of morality that's based on ethics, not on their bodies.

It's high time to do away with outdated—and dangerous—notions of virginity. If young women's only ethical gauge is based on whether they're chaste, we're ensuring that they will continue to define themselves by their sexuality.

In *The Purity Myth,* I not only discuss what the purity myth is and reveal its consequences for women, but also outline a new way for us to think about young women as moral actors, one that doesn't include their bodies. Not just because we deserve as much, but also because our health, our emotional well-being, and even our lives depend on it.

CHAPTER 1

the cult of virginity

"He said it was men invented virginity
not women. Father said it's like death:
only a state in which others are left ..."
WILLIAM FAULKNER,
The Sound and the Fury

IN THE MOMENTS AFTER I FIRST HAD SEX, my then-boyfriend—
lying down next to me over his lint-covered blanket—grabbed a pen from his
nightstand and drew a heart on the wall molding above his bed with our ini-
tials and the date inside. The only way you could see it was by lying flat on the
bed with your head smashed up against the wall. Crooked necks aside, it was a
sweet gesture, one that I'd forgotten about until I started writing this book.

The date seemed so important to us at the time, even though the event
itself was hardly awe-inspiring. There was the expected fumbling, a joke
about his fish-printed boxers, and ensuing condom difficulties. At one point,
his best friend even called to see how things were going. I suppose romance
and discretion are lost on sixteen-year-olds from Brooklyn. Yet we celebrated

our "anniversary" every year until we broke up, when Josh left for college two years before me and met a girl with a lip ring.

I've often wondered what that date marks—the day I became a woman? Considering I still bought underwear in cutesy three-packs, and that I certainly hadn't mastered the art of speaking my mind, I've gotta go with no. Societal standards would have me believe that it was the day I became morally sullied, but I fail to see how anything that lasts less than five minutes can have such an indelible ethical impact—so it's not that, either.

Really, the only meaning it had (besides a little bit of pain and a lot of postcoital embarrassment) was the meaning that Josh and I ascribed to it. Or so I thought. I hadn't counted on the meaning my peers, my parents, and society would imbue it with on my behalf.

From that date on—in the small, incestuous world of high school friendships, nothing is a secret for long—I was a "sexually active teen," a term often used in tandem with phrases like "at risk," or alongside warnings about drug and alcohol use, regardless of how uncontroversial the sex itself may have been. Through the rest of high school, whenever I had a date, my peers assumed that I had had sex because my sexuality had been defined by that one moment when my virginity was lost. It meant that I was no longer discriminating, no longer "good." The perceived change in my social value wasn't lost on my parents, either; before I graduated high school, my mother found an empty condom wrapper in my bag and remarked that if I kept having sex, no one would want to marry me.*

I realize that my experience isn't necessarily representative of most women's—everyone has their own story—but there are common themes in

---

* After years of denying she ever said such a thing, to her benefit, my mother finally sheepishy apologized.

so many young women's sexual journeys. Sometimes it's shame. Sometimes it's violence. Sometimes it's pleasure. And sometimes it's simply nothing to write home about.

The idea that virginity (or loss thereof) can profoundly affect women's lives is certainly nothing new. But what virginity is, what it was, and how it's being used now to punish women and roll back their rights is at the core of the purity myth. Because today, in a world where porn culture and reenergized abstinence movements collide, the moral panic myth about young women's supposed promiscuity is diverting attention from the real problem—that women are still being judged (sometimes to death) on something that doesn't really exist: virginity.

THE VIRGINITY MYSTERY

Before Hanne Blank wrote her book *Virgin: The Untouched History,* she had a bit of a problem. Blank was answering teens' questions on Scarleteen[1]—a sex-education website she founded with writer Heather Corinna so that young people could access information about sex online, other than porn and Net Nanny—when she discovered that she kept hitting a roadblock when it came to the topic of virginity.

"One of the questions that kept coming up was 'I did such-and-such. Am I still a virgin?'" Blank told me in an interview. "They desperately wanted an authoritative answer."

But she just didn't have one. So Blank decided to spend some time in Harvard's medical school library to find a definitive answer for her young web browsers.

"I spent about a week looking through everything I could—medical dictionaries, encyclopedias, anatomies—trying to find some sort of diagnostic standard for virginity," Blank said.

The problem was, there was no standard. Either a book wouldn't mention virginity at all or it would provide a definition that wasn't medical, but subjective.

"Then it dawned on me—I'm in arguably one of the best medical libraries in the world, scouring their stacks, and I'm not finding anything close to a medical definition for virginity. And I thought, *That's really weird. That's just flat-out strange.*"

Blank said she found it odd mostly because everyone, including doctors, talks about virginity as if they know what it is—but no one ever bothers to mention the truth: "People have been talking authoritatively about virginity for thousands of years, yet we don't even have a working medical definition for it!"

Blank now refers to virginity as "the state of having not had partnered sex." But if virginity is simply the first time someone has sex, then what is sex? If it's just heterosexual intercourse, then we'd have to come to the fairly ridiculous conclusion that all lesbians and gay men are virgins, and that different kinds of intimacy, like oral sex, mean nothing. And even using the straight-intercourse model of sex as a gauge, we'd have to get into the down-and-dirty conversation of what constitutes penetration.*

Since I've become convinced that virginity is a sham being perpetrated against women, I decided to turn to other people to see how they "count" sex. Most say it's penetration. Some say it's oral sex. My closest friend, Kate, a lesbian, has the best answer to date (a rule I've followed since she shared it with

---

* My college roommate Jen and I, I'm somewhat ashamed to admit, had a three pumps or more rule. Less than three pumps? You didn't have to count it as sex. We thought it was genius, as the three pump chumps, as we called them, were not necessarily the guys you wanted to remember.

me): It isn't sex unless you've had an orgasm. That's a pleasure-based, non-heter-onormative way of marking intimacy if I've ever heard one. Of course, this way of defining sex isn't likely to be very popular among the straight-male sect, given that some would probably end up not counting for many of their partners.

But any way you cut it, virginity is just too subjective to pretend we can define it.

Laura Carpenter, a professor at Vanderbilt University and the author of *Virginity Lost: An Intimate Portrait of First Sexual Experiences,* told me that when she wrote her book, she was loath to even use the word "virginity," lest she propagate the notion that there's one concrete definition for it.[2]

"What is this thing, this social phenomenon? I think the emphasis put on virginity, particularly for women, causes a lot more harm than good," said Carpenter.[3]

This has much to do with the fact that "virgin" is almost always synonymous with "woman." Virgin sacrifices, popping cherries, white dresses, supposed vaginal tightness, you name it. Outside of the occasional reference to the male virgin in the form of a goofy movie about horny teenage boys, virginity is pretty much all about women. Even the dictionary definitions of "virgin" cite an "unmarried girl or woman" or a "religious woman, esp. a saint."[4] No such definition exists for men or boys.

It's this inextricable relationship between sexual purity and women—how we're either virgins or not virgins—that makes the very concept of virginity so dangerous and so necessary to do away with.

Admittedly, it would be hard to dismiss virginity as we know it altogether, considering the meaning it has in so many people's—especially women's—lives. When I suggest that virginity is a lie told to women, I don't aim to discount or make light of how important the current social idea of virginity is for some people. Culture, religion, and social beliefs influence the role that virginity and sexuality play in women's lives—sometimes very positively. So, to be clear, when I argue for an end to the idea of virginity, it's because I believe sexual intimacy should be honored and respected, but that it shouldn't be revered at the expense of women's well-being, or seen as such an integral part of female identity that we end up defining ourselves by our sexuality.

I also can't discount that no matter what personal meaning each woman gives virginity, it's people who have social and political influence who ultimately get to decide what virginity means—at least, as it affects women on a large scale.

VIRGINITY: COMMODITY, MORALITY, OR FARCE?

It's hard to know when people started caring about virginity, but we do know that men, or male-led institutions, have always been the ones that get to define and assign value to virginity.

Blank posits that a long-standing historical interest in virginity is about establishing paternity (if a man marries a virgin, he can be reasonably sure the child she bears is his) and about using women's sexuality as a commodity. Either way, the notion has always been deeply entrenched in patriarchy and male ownership.

> Raising daughters of quality became another model of production, as valuable as breeding healthy sheep, weaving sturdy cloth, or bringing in a good harvest. ... The gesture is now generally symbolic in the first world, but we nonetheless still observe the custom of the father "giving" his daughter in marriage. Up until the last century or so, however, when laws were liberalized to allow women to stand as full citizens in their own right, this represented a literal transfer of property from a father's household to a husband's.[5]

That's why women who had sex were (and still are, at times) referred to as "damaged goods"—because they were literally just that: something to be owned, traded, bought, and sold.

But long gone are the days when women were property . . . or so we'd like to think. It's not just wedding traditions or outdated laws that name women's virginity as a commodity; women's virginity, our sexuality, is still assigned a value by a movement with more power and influence in American society than we'd probably like to admit.

I like to call this movement the virginity movement.* And it is a movement, indeed—with conservatives and evangelical Christians at the helm, and our government, school systems, and social institutions taking orders. Composed of antifeminist think tanks like the Independent Women's Forum and Concerned Women for America; abstinence-only "educators" and organizations; religious leaders; and legislators with regressive social values, the virginity movement is much more than just the same old sexism; it's a targeted and well-funded backlash that is rolling back women's rights using revamped and modernized definitions of purity, morality, and sexuality. Its goals are mired in old-school gender roles, and the tool it's using is young women's sexuality. (What better way to get people to pay attention to your cause than to frame it in terms of teenage girls' having, or not having, sex? It's salacious!)

And, like it or not, the members of the virginity movement are the people who are defining virginity—and, to a large extent, sexuality—in America. Now, instead of women's virginity being explicitly bought and

---

* The "abstinence movement" would be accurate, as would the "chastity movement." But neither quite captures how this obsession really is about virginity, virgins, and an almost too-enthusiastic focus on young women's sexuality. So the "virginity movement" seemed not only appropriate, but also a bit needling. Which I enjoy.

sold with dowries and business deals, it's being defined as little more than a stand-in for actual morality.

It's genius, really. Shame women into being chaste and tell them that all they have to do to be "good" is not have sex. (Of course, chastity and purity, as defined by the virginity movement, are not just about abstaining sexually so much as they're about upholding a specific, passive model of womanhood. But more on this later.)

For women especially, virginity has become the easy answer—the morality quick fix. You can be vapid, stupid, and unethical, but so long as you've never had sex, you're a "good" (i.e., "moral") girl and therefore worthy of praise.

Present-day American society—whether through pop culture, religion, or institutions—conflates sexuality and morality constantly. Idolizing virginity as a stand-in for women's morality means that nothing else matters— not what we accomplish, not what we think, not what we care about and work for. Just if/how/whom we have sex with. That's all.

Just look at the women we venerate for not having sex: pageant queens who run on abstinence platforms, pop singers who share their virginal status, and religious women who "save themselves" for marriage. It's an interesting state of affairs when women have to simply do, well, *nothing* in order to be considered ethical role models. As Feministing.com commenter electron-Blue noted in response to the 2008 *New York Times Magazine* article "Students of Virginity," on abstinence clubs at Ivy League colleges, "There were a WHOLE LOTTA us not having sex at Harvard . . . but none of us thought that that was special enough to start a club about it, for pete's sake."[6]

But for plenty of women across the country, it *is* special. Staying "pure" and "innocent" is touted as the greatest thing we can do. However, equating this inaction with morality not only is problematic because it continues to tie women's ethics to our bodies, but also is downright insulting because it suggests that women can't be moral actors. Instead, we're defined by what we don't do—our ethics are the ethics of passivity. (This model of ethics fits in perfectly with how the virginity movement defines the ideal woman.)

Proponents of chastity and abstinence, though, would have us believe that abstaining indeed requires strength and action. Janie Fredell, one of the students quoted in the above-mentioned *New York Times Magazine* piece, penned a college newspaper article claiming that virginity is "rooted . . . in the notion of strength."

"It takes a strong woman to be abstinent, and that's the sort of woman I want to be," Fredell told the magazine.[7] Her rhetoric of strength is part of a growing trend among the conservative virginity-fetish sect, which is likely the result of virginity movement leaders seeing how questionable the "passive virgin" is in modern society. Now we're seeing virginity proponents assert their fortitude. Conservative messages aimed at young men even call on them to be "virginity warriors," driving home the message that it's men's responsibility to safeguard virginity for their female counterparts, simultaneously quashing any fears of feminization that boys may have surrounding abstinence.

Perhaps it's true that in our sex-saturated culture, it does take a certain amount of self-discipline to resist having sex, but restraint does not equal morality. And let's be honest: If this were simply about resisting peer pressure and being strong, then the women who have sex because they actively want to—as appalling as that idea might be to those who advocate abstinence—wouldn't be scorned. Because the "strength" involved in these women's choice would be about doing what they want despite pressure to the contrary, not about resisting the sex act itself. But women who have sex are often denigrated by those who revere virginity. As feminist blogger Jill Filipovic noted in response to Fredell:

> I appreciate and applaud the personal strength of individuals who decide abstinence is the best choice for them. But what I can't support is the constant attacks on sexually active people. People who have sex do not feel a constant need to tell abstinent people that their human dignity has been compromised, or that they're dirty, or that they are secretly unhappy, or that they're headed for total life ruin.[8]

And that is exactly what young women are taught, thanks in no small part to conservative backlash. In 2005, for example, the evangelical Christian group Focus on the Family came out with a study reporting that having sex before the age of eighteen makes you more likely to end up poor and divorced.[9] Given that the median age for sexual initiation for all Americans—male and female—is seventeen, I wonder how shocked most women will be when they learn that they have a life of poverty-stricken spinsterhood to look forward to!

But it's not only abstinence education or conservative propaganda that are perpetuating this message; you need look no further than pop culture for stark examples of how young people—especially young women—are taught to use virginity as an easy ethical road map.

A 2007 episode of the MTV documentary series *True Life* featured celibate youth.[10] Among the teens choosing to abstain because of disease concerns and religious commitments was nineteen-year-old Kristin from Nashville, Tennessee. Kristin had cheated on her past boyfriends, and told the camera she'd decided to remain celibate until she feels she can be faithful to her current boyfriend. Clearly, Kristin's problem isn't sex—it's trust. But instead of dealing with the actual issues behind her relationship woes, this young woman was able to circumvent any real self-analysis by simply claiming to be abstinent. So long as she's chaste, she's good.

Or consider singer and reality television celebrity Jessica Simpson, who has made her career largely by playing on the sexy-virgin stereotype. Simpson, the daughter of a Baptist youth minister, started her singing career by touring Christian youth festivals and True Love Waits events. Even when she went mainstream, she publicly declared her virginity—stating that her father had given her a promise ring when she was twelve years old—and spoke of her intention to wait to have sex until marriage. Meanwhile, not surprisingly, Simpson was being marketed as a major sex symbol—all blond hair, breasts, and giggles. Especially giggles. Simpson's character (and I use the word "character" because it's hard to know what was actually her and not a finely honed image) was sold as the archetypal dumb blond. Thoughtless moments on *Newlyweds,* the MTV show that followed her short-lived marriage to singer Nick Lachey, became nationally known sound bites, such as Simpson's wondering aloud whether tuna was chicken or fish, since the can read "Chicken of the Sea."

Despite Simpson's public persona as an airhead (as recently as 2008, she was featured in a Macy's commercial as not understanding how to flick on a light switch), women are supposed to want to be her, not only because she's beautiful by conventional standards, but also because she adheres to the social structures that tell women that they exist purely for men: as a virgin, as a sex symbol, or, in Simpson's case, as both. It doesn't matter that Simpson reveals few of her actual thoughts or moral beliefs; it's enough that she's "pure," even if that purity means she's a bit of a dolt.

For those women who can't keep up the front as well as someone like Simpson, they suffer heaps of judgment—especially when they fall off the pedestal they're posed upon so perfectly. American pop culture, especially, has an interesting new trend of venerating and fetishizing "pure" young women—whether they're celebrities, beauty queens, or just everyday young women—simply to bask in their eventual fall.

And no one embodies the "perfect" young American woman like beauty queens. They're pretty, overwhelmingly white, thin, and eager to please.* And, of course, pageant queens are supposed to be as pure as pure can be. In fact, until 1999, the Miss America pageant had a "purity rule" that barred divorced women and those who had obtained abortions from entering the contest—lest they sully the competition, I suppose.[11]

So in 2006, when two of those "perfect" girls made the news for being in scandalous photos on the Internet, supposed promiscuity, or a combination thereof, Americans were transfixed.

First, twenty-year-old Miss USA Tara Conner was nearly stripped of her title after reports surfaced that she frequented nightclubs, drank, and dated. Hardly unusual behavior for a young woman, regardless of how many tiaras she may have.

The *New York Daily News* could barely contain its slut-shaming glee when it reported on the story: "'She really is a small-town girl. She just went wild when she came to the city,' one nightlife veteran said. 'Tara just couldn't handle herself. They were sneaking those [nightclub] guys in and out of the

---

* Who, after all, can maintain a pearly white perma-grin through humiliating bathing suit competitions and inane questions—all for scholarships that are paltry in comparison to the money spent on gowns and coaches—other than women looking for some serious validation?

apartment' . . . Conner still brought boyfriends home. . . . Soon she broke up with her hometown fiancé and started dating around in the Manhattan night-club world. . . . "[12]

Instead of having her crown taken away, however, Conner was publicly "forgiven" by Miss USA co-owner Donald Trump, who appeared at a press conference to publicly declare he was giving the young woman a second chance.[13] In case you had any doubts about whether this controversy was all tied up with male ownership and approval, consider the fact that Trump later reportedly considered giving his permission for Conner to pose for *Playboy* magazine. He played the role of dad, pimp, and owner, all rolled into one.[14]

Mere days later, Miss Nevada USA, twenty-two-year-old Katie Rees, was dethroned after pictures of her exposing one of her breasts and mooning the camera were uncovered.[15] When you're on a pedestal, you have a long way to fall.

And, of course, it's impossible to talk about tipped-over pedestals without mentioning pop singer Britney Spears. Spears, first made famous by her hit song "Baby One More Time" and its accompanying video, in which she appeared in a Catholic schoolgirl mini-uniform, was very much the American purity princess. She publicly declared her virginity and belief in abstinence before marriage, all the while being marketed—much like Simpson was—as a sex symbol. But unlike Simpson, Spears fell far from grace in the eyes of the American public. The most obvious indications of her decline were splashed across newspapers and entertainment weeklies worldwide—a breakdown during which she shaved her head in front of photographers, and various pictures of her drunk and sans panties. But Spears began distancing herself from the virgin ideal long before these incidents hit the tabloids.

First, Spears got some press for moving in with then-boyfriend and fellow pop star Justin Timberlake. But the sexist brouhaha began in earnest when Spears was no longer considered "attractive," because she started to gain weight, got pregnant, and no longer looked like a little girl. Pictures of her cellulite popped up on websites and gossip magazines nationwide, along with guesstimations about her weight and jokes about her stomach. Because "purity" isn't just about not having sex, it's about not being a woman—and instead being in a state of perpetual girlhood (more on this in Chapter 3).

Shaming young women for being sexual is nothing new, but it's curious to observe how the expectation of purity gets played out through the women who are supposed to epitomize the feminine ideal: the "desirable" virgin. After all, we rarely see women who aren't conventionally beautiful idolized for their abstinence. And no matter how "good" you are otherwise—even if you're an all-American beauty queen—if you're not virginal, you're shamed.

The desirable virgin is sexy but not sexual. She's young, white, and skinny. She's a cheerleader, a baby sitter; she's accessible and eager to please (remember those ethics of passivity!). She's never a woman of color. She's never a low-income girl or a fat girl. She's never disabled. "Virgin" is a designation for those who meet a certain standard of what women, especially younger women, are supposed to look like. As for how these young women are supposed to act? A blank slate is best.

SELLING VIRGINITY

Unfortunately, this morality model of virginity—in which women's morals and ethical ability are defined solely by their sexual status—isn't the only type the virginity movement is pushing. Viewing virginity as a commodity—as it was seen back in the days in which daughters were exchanged as property—lives on, just in less obvious ways (though, arguably, much more insidiously).

Now fathers participate in purity balls and virginity pledges to maintain ownership over their daughters, even if it's only symbolic. Women's sexuality is still very much for sale.

Not so shockingly to those of us who do feminist and progressive political work, the conservative, religious right has been at the center of keeping women's bodies on the market. The backlash against women's rights over the past three decades has ranged from rolling back our reproductive rights to launching antisexuality scare-tactic campaigns—all part of a larger concerted effort desperately seeking a return to traditional gender roles. Make no mistake about it—these efforts are at the heart of the virginity movement and its goals.

And they've been successful. To a large extent, the virginity movement is the new authority on sexuality. It's in our schools, telling our children what sex is (dirty, wrong, and dangerous), and in our homes, creating legislation that violates women's privacy and bodies (more on this in Chapter 6).

In addition to promoting the virginity-as-morality model, the virginity movement is working hard to reaffirm virginity as something to be bought, sold, and owned. Sometimes these attempts transpire in more obvious ways than others.

Take, for example, Virginity Vouchers. Sold to abstinence educators as abstinence commitment cards to hand out to students, these vouchers, which look much like credit cards, feature a background image of a bride and groom with the words VIRGINITY VOUCHER: DON'T BUY THE LIE, SAVE SEX FOR MARRIAGE emblazoned across it. The Abstinence Clearinghouse, the largest and best-known abstinence education nonprofit organization in the country, sells the card on its website and makes no effort to hide the fact that this product is, quite literally, commodifying virginity:

This "Virginity Voucher" is a hard plastic commitment card with a place on the back to sign their name. Created for both young men and women, this card can be kept in their wallet to remind them of their decision![16]

Right along with their MasterCards and Visas!

Or consider another abstinence product: a gold rose pin handed out in schools and at Christian youth events. The pin is attached to a small card that reads, "You are like a beautiful rose. Each time you engage in pre-marital sex, a precious petal is stripped away. Don't leave your future husband holding a bare stem. Abstain."[17]

Do we really want to teach our daughters that without their virginity, they're nothing but a "bare stem"?

Abstinence-only education (see Chapter 5), which receives more than $178 million a year in federal funding, is chock full of lessons like these that tell students that female sexuality is a "gift," "precious," and something to "save."

A 2008 advertisement promoting Abstinence Awareness Week in Washington, D.C., told young women to "guard your diamond" alongside a picture of a tremendous gem covered in chains and a lock.[18]

And, of course, there are purity balls—the federally funded father/daughter dances where girls as young as age six pledge their virginity to their dads, who in turn pledge to hang on to said virginity until an appropriate husband comes along, to whom the fathers can transfer ownership of their daughters.

Not all of the virginity-for-sale messages are so overt, but all of them are sexist and all of them are dangerous. Why? Because if virginity is a gift, or something "worth saving," that means that those who don't save it are somehow lacking—or, even worse, sullied.

Sex-as-dirty and women-as-tainted messages are central to the virginity movement and are perpetuated most visibly in the most unfortunate of places—our schools. The primary perpetrator, abstinence-only education, has established programs across the country to tell young women that they're somehow spoiled by sex.

One popular classroom exercise, for example, employs Scotch Tape to demonstrate how premarital sex can make girls dirty.* A teacher holds up a clear strip of tape, meant to represent a girl, in front of the class. The teacher then puts the strip of tape, adhesive side down, on the arm of a boy in the class, to symbolize his sexual relationship with the girl. The teacher rips off the tape (signifying the breakup, apparently) and holds it up again for the class to look at. Students are meant to see that the strip of tape—the girl—has picked up all kinds of dirt and hair from the boy's arm and is no longer clean. Then, when the teacher tries to stick the same strip of tape to another boy's arm, he or she notes that it doesn't stick—they can't bond! To end things with a bang, the abstinence educator makes a remark about the girl's being "used" and therefore unable to have strong future relationships.[19]

In another popular exercise, abstinence teachers' use candy to make their "dirty" points. These candy exercises often consist of teachers' showing how the candy can't fit back into its wrapper after being chewed/sucked/eaten. Another program in Nevada even used its abstinence-only state funding to run public radio service ads that said girls will feel "dirty and cheap" after having sex. (The ads were later pulled due to listener outrage.[20]) The fact that these examples nearly always focus on girls is no coincidence. After all, our bodies are the ones that get objectified and pathologized, and it's our morality that's supposedly in jeopardy.

---

* Most classroom exercises focus on girls and their potential filthiness.

But sullied students across America shouldn't fret! The virginity movement has ensured that there's a way out of the dirt trap: Megan Landry of Houma, Louisiana, signed a "Pure Love Promise" commitment card when she was sixteen years old while attending Abbey Youth Fest, a Louisiana event for young Catholics. The card, which she signed, dated, and carried in her wallet, reads, "Believing that sex is sacred, I promise to God that I will save the gift of my sexuality from now until marriage. I choose to glorify God with my body and pursue a life of purity, trusting that the Lord is never outdone in generosity."[21]

As it turns out, Landry had already lost her virginity to a boyfriend when she was in the tenth grade, but she was moved to sign the card anyway after hearing one of the event speakers, Jason Evert, author of *Pure Love*.

"[Evert] gave a talk about purity and saving yourself for marriage. He told us about how he had waited until he was married for sex, but his fiancée had already slept with someone. They both decided to not sleep with each other—he took a pledge and his girlfriend took a secondary virginity pledge. I just thought that was sooooo sweeeet," Landry wrote in an email to me.

The notion of secondary virginity—that you can regain your spiritual and emotional purity by pledging abstinence until marriage, no matter what your sexual history—first became popular in the mid-1980s among conservative Christian groups.[22] Also called born-again virginity, the notion is widespread in Christian programs for young people, abstinence-only education, and even pop culture.

Perhaps sensing that the number of teen virgins in the United States was diminishing, religious groups saw secondary virginity as their opportunity to (for lack of a better term) put more asses in the seats. What better way to increase the numbers of virginity pledgers than to open up the process to everyone—even the promiscuous! It's possible that the virginity movement even recognized that the purity standard of not having intercourse was simply unrealistic, and saw how promoting a promise that focused on emotional and spiritual purity might woo those who felt ostracized by their virginityless status.

What I find interesting about secondary virginity is that while it may seem like an easy out, with its emphasis on emotional and spiritual purity, it actually takes a hardline approach to chastity and has the effect of increasing the obstacles to being pure. After all, to be a virgin, all you have to do is not have sex. But to fully embrace your secondary virginity, you must abstain not only from intercourse, but also from masturbation or even thinking about sex. And there's no more of this "anything but" nonsense, either—Love Matters, a teen abstinence program, tells those considering being secondary virgins to "avoid intense hugging," and that "anything beyond a brief, simple kiss can quickly become dangerous."[23]

Some groups even advise women to change the way they act and dress to convey their chastity appropriately. An article from Focus on the Family, "Pure Again," notes that "women find they want to try a different way of dressing—to show more respect for their own bodies."*[24]

Despite efforts to link secondary virginity to teens' emotional and spiritual selves, the virginity movement's obsession with bodily purity is impossible to hide. Undercutting the movement's argument that purity is about spirituality is the fact that many of the secondary-virginity and chastity messages come from crisis pregnancy centers, groups that masquerade

---

* As with most things in the virginity movement, there's a lot of lip service when it comes to young men and secondary or born-again virginity, but the focus remains on women.

as medical clinics when their actual purpose is to convince young women not to have abortions. What could be more intimately tied with women's bodies and sexuality than pregnancy? And, let's face it, the language of secondary virginity isn't exactly subtle. On the website for A Pregnancy Resource Center of Northeast Ohio, an article titled "Take2" asks, "Have you already unwrapped the priceless gift of virginity and given it away? Do you now feel like 'second-hand goods' and no longer worthy to be cherished? Do you ever wish you could re-wrap it and give it only to your future husband or wife?"[25]

But not to worry, there's an answer! "Guess what? You can be abstinent again! You can't change the past, but you can change the future. You can decide today to commit to abstinence, wrapping a brand-new gift of virginity to present to your husband or wife on your wedding night."[26]

The message is clear: Without your "gift," you're "second-hand goods." (Or at least, if you're properly repentant, that's what you should feel like.)

Like most virginity pledges, the appeal of secondary virginity doesn't seem to last long. Landry, the secondary virginity–pledging teen from Louisiana, broke her pledge within the year:

> As the months went by, I gradually stopped hanging out with my religious friends and got a serious boyfriend," she said. "About eight months after I signed the pledge, on New Year's Eve, I had no use for that card anymore. We dated for about one month before we had sex. After this relationship, I had no interest in abstinence and purity pledges. I was over it.

Landry is not alone in being "over it." Like first-time virginity pledgers, secondary virginity pledgers are likely to abandon their promise, and even more likely to not use contraception.* Another young virginity pledger, Emily Seipel of Michigan, even told me that her high school virginity pledge was "an easy [way] to resist flesh sins when you're already a closeted lesbian." (Gay people don't exist in the virginity movement, remember?) Seipel, who is technically still a virgin by conventional standards, is far from alone. The purity that the virginity movement is working so hard for is more of an illusion than it would like to own up to. Teens who make these pledges often do so in front of church members, peers, parents, and community leaders, and oftentimes they have no real choice in the matter. It's not as if many twelve- to fourteen-year-olds are going to be self-assured enough to refuse to take a chastity vow. ("No thanks, Mom, I'd like to keep my sexual options open!") These pledges are little more than cultural farces created to make parents feel better about their children's coming of age. And, frankly, parents who buy into the purity myth need some hope; after all, mainstream media would have them believe that their daughters are going wild and are perhaps irredeemably tainted (more on this in Chapter 2).

Whether they're pledges, bare stems, or Virginity Vouchers, the messages are clearly regressive. But virginity proponents are doing one heck of a job marketing them as "revolutionary" and "empowering." Appropriating feminist rhetoric to reinforce traditional gender roles is nothing if not brilliant.

Wendy Shalit, a writer and virginity guru whose first book, *A Return to Modesty: Discovering Lost Virtue,* was the topic of much debate when it was released in 2000, is a prime player in the "making abstinence cool" movement (or, as she calls it, the "modesty movement"). Shalit, who in 2007 penned

---

* Contraception is for "bad" girls who planned out sex, not girls who got caught in the heat of the moment. And, of course, many of these teens are taught that birth control doesn't work anyway, so why bother?

another ode to chastity, *Girls Gone Mild: Young Women Reclaim Self-Respect and Find It's Not Bad to Be Good,* founded a website, the Modesty Zone,[27] and a blog, Modestly Yours,[28] which has twenty-one in-house bloggers. The site describes itself as "an informal community of young women who don't have a voice in the mainstream media."

"Whether you're a virgin waiting until marriage, or just against casual sex more generally, you can find a safe harbour here to share your ideals, interests, and goals for the future," it reads. The Modesty Zone features "Rebels of the Month" and slogans like "Be Daring, keep your shirt on!" Of course, the core message of the modesty movement is still in plain view, as evidenced by the blog's tagline: "Modesty Zone: A site for good girls."

Some virginity-movement members are even resorting to using sex to sell their antisex message. A shirt being sold on the website of the Heritage Foundation, a conservative Christian organization, says, VIRGINS ARE HOT, and groups on Facebook dedicated to the same message call their own work "passion for purity."

What's most telling about all of these efforts, whether they're being executed via education, religion, or social imperatives, is that they're not working—at least, not in the ways the movement would like them to. Virginity pledges have proved ineffective time and time again; the same is true of abstinence-only education.[29] Blogs like Shalit's Modesty Zone have little web traffic,[30] and the purity groups on social-networking sites are dwarfed by groups like "This is what a feminist looks like" or even those as trivial as "If You Can't Differentiate Between 'Your' and 'You're' You Deserve To Die."

Despite its inability to keep women "pure," or to convince most Americans that abstinence is best, the virginity movement is strong, well funded, and everywhere. While there isn't a critical mass of young people who identify with this movement, that doesn't mean they aren't affected by it; these are the people who are teaching our kids about sex and teaching our daughters about morality. And what they're teaching them is wrong.

Abstinence-only classes are part of the reason why one in four young American women have a sexually transmitted infection (STI),[31] and are certainly to blame for the disturbing revelation that teens in Florida believe drinking a cap of bleach will prevent HIV, and a shot of Mountain Dew will stop pregnancy.[32] These are the organizations with billboards peppered across America's highways telling young women, WAIT FOR THE BLING and THE ULTIMATE WEDDING GIFT IS YOUR VIRGINITY.[33]

All of these messages—which position certain young women as the ideal, substitute sexual purity for real morality, and commodify virginity—are part of a larger effort to roll back all women's rights. The virginity movement is seeking a return to traditional gender roles, and focusing on purity is the vehicle toward that end.

When I emailed my high school ex to let him know about this book, I asked him about our first time and what he took away from the experience. Like mine, his memories were wrought with uncomfortable moments* and questions. He remembers writing the date above his bed as a way to add permanence to a fleeting moment. I was surprised to learn, however, that his views about women's sexuality weren't any more sophisticated than what I remembered them to be during our teenage years.

"No matter how sexually curious or 'ready' a girl is, she seems to be able to keep her wits about her a bit better than her male counterparts, so more is expected of [women], and rightly so," Josh wrote to me. This is an all-too-

---

* Like his trying to hold back by staring at a bottle of Drakkar Noir cologne and attempting to spell the name backward.

common assertion—the idea that women are somehow less sexual than men and are therefore the gatekeepers of sexual morals. It's a fundamental notion of the virginity movement, however, so I shouldn't have been so shocked to hear this line of reasoning being regurgitated by my former boyfriend. After all, the purity message is widespread. But it's one thing to hear the media use this type of language about Britney Spears; it was quite another to hear an ex-boyfriend use it about me. At the end of the day, though, it *is* about me—it's about all of us. However theoretically we'd like to discuss issues of virginity, purity, and women's moral value, the fact is, they affect all of us.

CHAPTER 2

tainted love

"Your body is a wrapped lollipop. When you have sex with a man, he unwraps your lollipop and sucks on it. It may feel great at the time, but, unfortunately, when he's done with you, all you have left for your next partner is a poorly wrapped, saliva-fouled sucker."

DARREN WASHINGTON,
an abstinence educator at the Eighth Annual
Abstinence Clearinghouse Conference[1]

THE ABOVE QUOTE IS ONE I REPEAT often when speaking at colleges and feminist events. It's shocking, telling, and, frankly, disgusting. Unfortunately, it also epitomizes the message that the virginity movement is working so hard to send to women: Sex makes us less whole and a whole lot dirtier.

I've never understood what it is about having sex that makes women dirty. I can recall countless conversations I've had or overhead over the years about women's supposed sexual dirtiness. Struggling with the irrationality of it all, I've often wondered how it's possible that a penis could have such power, that by merely being in the *vicinity* of a woman's genitals, it could transfer some kind of ambiguous filth onto us. Or perhaps women are just *born* dirty, and the sex merely reinforces our sullied selves' true nature.

When I've gotten engaged enough to argue commonsense points about the sexual double standard—Aren't men sullied as well? If you use a condom, are you less dirty because you don't actually come in contact with the penis?—I've been met with refutations, mostly from men, about how women who are willing to "give it up" easily aren't really the datable kind anyway.

The men I've had these conversations with, misguided as they were, had to have absorbed this line of thinking somewhere. And I can't say I completely fault them, since popular culture is saturated with ever more sexual images while sexuality is still being touted simultaneously as dirty, wrong, and even deadly. The messages that sex for anything other than procreation makes women used goods are disproportionately targeted toward girls and young women, but the impact they have on boys and young men is equally harmful. While girls internalize this message, boys are propagating and enforcing it.

So where does it come from, this dirty double standard? Pathologizing women's bodies and sexuality is certainly nothing new; from "hysteria"* to fears about menstruation, women have been considered the "dirtier" sex for a long time.

In *The Female Thing,* author Laura Kipnis argues that fear of women's bodies, specifically our genitals, is at the heart of the dirt double standard.

> *Recall the unhappy fact that throughout history there's been the universal conviction that women are somehow dirtier than men. The male body is regarded, or is symbolically, as cleaner than the female body. . . . Possibly it's that outjutting parts of the body, like a penis, are regarded as somehow cleaner than holes and cavities. . . . The vagina is frequently associated with rot and decay. . . . [2]*

* The word "hysteria" actually comes from the antiquated idea that women's emotional problems were derived from the uterus.

Not exactly the kind of message we'd like to see spread around, yet that's what we're stuck with. Educators, religious leaders, media, and parents alike help to promote these notions of dirty girls. Headlines about girls "gone wild" dominate newspapers and wire services, STI rates are discussed alongside stories of supposedly promiscuous teens on cable news shows, and books about the "hookup culture" ruining young women are a dime a dozen. The scare tactics are everywhere and the message is the same: Sex is hurting women.

Sex for pleasure, for fun, or even for building relationships is completely absent from our national conversation. Yet taking the joy out of sexuality is a surefire way to ensure not that young women won't have sex, but rather that they'll have it without pleasure.*

PERFECT VIRGINS, DIRTY GIRLS

The Abstinence Clearinghouse's website is a virtual cornucopia of virginity worship.[3] It features educational tools, videos, a blog, pictures of purity balls, and links to conservative and religious organizations, all touting purity and chastity. The website also features a page where women (and only women) are pictured and quoted about why they're chaste. One such quote, from sixteen-year-old Ashley Dial of Tampa, Florida, reads, "I don't want to show up empty-handed on my wedding night. I want to have the whole package to give to my husband and my husband only."

Jolene Churchill of Evansville, Wisconsin, says, "Whenever I get the opportunity to speak to young people, I beg them not to become another broken victim of the lie of safe sex. The loss of one's self-esteem, health, and

---

* Pleasure is widely dismissed, if not denounced, in the virginity movement. When the purpose of sex is simply procreation, pleasure is simply gratuitous.

potentially their life is just too high of a price tag to pay for merely being used by another individual."*4

When did sex become such a downer?! "The whole package"? "Broken victim"? These are fighting words for those of us who see sex as a healthy expression. Would it be so terrible to talk about sex in a way that acknowledges how wonderful it can be?

After all, it's not as if the virginity movement is completely without joy. On the contrary, it finds happiness in discussing girls' virginity—in the form of its perfect virgins. Women like Churchill, Dial, and Janie Fredell, the young woman featured in The *New York Times Magazine* article who equated saving her virginity with strength, are held up by pro-virginity organizations as the ideal woman. They're quoted on websites and touted as "purity princesses,"5 and are the apples of their virginity-pledging fathers' eyes. But what happens when these pure teens get married and have sex? Are they still strong and joyful then? Presumably, but when the virginity movement speaks of sexual joy within marriages, that joy is not about orgasms or intimacy; it's about the (almost smirking) knowledge that your relationship is more "complete" than other people's *because* you waited.†

It makes sense—after all, the perfect virgin and holding up examples of chaste young women are integral to the virginity movement. The problem with this, however, aside from the way it fetishizes young women's sexuality, is that the girls presented as examples by the virginity movement are by and large a narrow, idealized representation: young, good-looking, straight, and white.

---

* Interestingly enough, a Google search reveals that Churchill is on staff with the Wisconsin state legislature—the virginity movement is not just on abstinence websites, they're affecting policy!

† Holier-than-thou joy in sex is just not something I can stand behind, no matter how good it is.

Young women of color, who are so hypersexualized in American culture that they're rarely positioned as "the virgin" in the virginity movement or elsewhere, are largely absent from discourse concerning chastity. How can you be "pure" if you are seen as dirty to begin with?

As bell hooks wrote in a 1998 essay, "Naked Without Shame," about black women's bodies and politics, "Marked by shame, projected as inherent and therefore precluding any possibility of innocence, the black female body was beyond redemption."[6] She points out that since the time of U.S. slavery, men have benefited from positioning black women as naturally promiscuous because it absolves them of guilt when they sexually assault and rape women of color. "[I]t was impossible to ruin that which was received as inherently unworthy, tainted, and soiled," hooks wrote.[7]

Women of color, low-income women, immigrant women—these are the women who are not seen as worthy of being placed on a pedestal. It's only our perfect virgins who are valuable, worthy of discourse and worship.

We're a sex divided. As Patricia Hill Collins once wrote, "Dividing women into two categories—the asexual, moral women to be protected by marriage and their sexual, immoral counterparts—served as a gender template for constructing ideas about masculinity and femininity."[8]

I'd also argue that merely positioning one kind of woman over all others as good and "clean" implies that the rest of us are dirty. So for those women who don't fall under the perfect-virgin category, schools, newspapers, and American culture in general are ready and waiting to tell them that they're impure.

MEDIA GONE WILD

If you spend any amount of time doing media analysis, it's clear that the most frenzied moral panic surrounding young women's sexuality comes from the mainstream media, which loves to report about how promiscuous girls are, whether they're acting up on spring break, getting caught topless on camera, or catching all kinds of STIs. Unsurprisingly, these types of articles and stories generally fail to mention that women are attending college at the highest rates in history, and that we're the majority of undergraduate and master's students. Well-educated and socially engaged women just don't make for good headlines, it seems.[9]

In 2007 alone, nearly one thousand articles referred to the "girls gone wild" and "raunch culture" phenomenon.[10] Topics ranged from general hawing about girls' promiscuity to the "trend" of bikini waxing for ten-year-olds[11] to bemoaning college women's "slutty" Halloween costumes.[12] A 2007 feature article for *Newsweek*, "Girls Gone Bad," even wondered whether America was raising a generation of "prosti-tots."[13]

This isn't to say that there isn't a real problem around the way young women are being oversexualized—of course there is. But media coverage focuses more on salacious scare tactics than on nuance. For example, a 2006 editorial in *The New York Times* titled "Middle School Girls Gone Wild," about so-called suggestive dancing in school performances, channels the hackneyed "these darn kids" trope, rather than actual discourse.

> *They writhe and strut, shake their bottoms, splay their legs, thrust their chests out and in and out again. Some straddle empty chairs, like lap dancers without laps. They don't smile much. Their faces are locked from grim exertion, from all that leaping up and lying down without poles to hold onto. 'Don't stop don't stop,' sings Janet Jackson, all whispery. 'Jerk it like you're making it choke . . . ohh. I'm so stimulated. Feel so X-rated.' The girls spend a lot of time lying on the floor. They are in the sixth, seventh, and eighth grades.[14]*

Rarely do editorials own up to the fact that "dirty dancing" has been around since the 1950s, when parents were up in arms about rock 'n' roll music.

And as for the question of *who's* being covered when we talk about promiscuity, disproportionately it's young white women. Why? Because the sexuality of young women of color—especially African Americans and Latinas—is never framed as "good girls gone bad"; rather, they're depicted as having some degree of pathologized sexuality from the get-go, no matter what their virginity status. You'll find articles about STI rates, pregnancy, and poverty—which *are* issues that affect women of color disproportionately and deserve attention. But when articles about the sexual infection rates of African American women are one column over from an article about young white women's spring break, a disturbing cultural narrative is reinforced—that "innocent" white girls are being lured into an oversexualized culture, while young black women are already part of it.

One of the most frustrating outcomes of this recent media panic is that it's produced more hand wringing and finger wagging than actual results. The only tangible outcome of the girls-gone-wild media trend is a handful of lucrative careers. After all, nothing makes money like lamenting fallen and promiscuous youth, especially when those youth are female.

Not to be outdone by wire services and news magazines, sex-scare writers have also started promoting purity with books. Modesty maven Wendy Shalit is not the only writer to gain from pushing chastity. In 2007, *five* popular books, all arguing that sexual activity hurts young women, were released: *Unhooked: How Young Women Pursue Sex, Delay Love and Lose at Both,* by Laura Sessions Stepp; *Prude: How the Sex-Obsessed Culture Hurts Young Women (and America, Too!),* by Carol Platt Liebau; *The Thrill of the Chaste:*

Finding Fulfillment While Keeping Your Clothes On, by Dawn Eden; *Unprotected: A Campus Psychiatrist Reveals How Political Correctness in Her Profession Endangers Every Student*, by Miriam Grossman; and, of course, *Girls Gone Mild*, by Wendy Shalit.

These books were written by virginity-movement frontliners, all using the media's obsession with young women's "deviant" sexuality to cash in and spread their regressive messages. I'll save you some money here, because these books can actually all be summed up in one sentence: If you're a young, unmarried woman who's having sex, you're putting yourself in danger—better go back to baking cookies and pretending you don't know what a clitoris is. (Really. I wish I were joking.) The only real difference I can determine among these books is *which* supposed consequence of women's sexuality the author chose to focus on. For Stepp, it's emotional consequences; for Grossman, physical. Shalit wrote about the moral implications of sexuality, and Eden, the spiritual. Liebau beat all them, however, with her argument that young women's engaging in sex has national political consequences! All of these supposed penalties have multiple tie-ins with other virginity-movement rhetoric and organizing—and all with the same goal: to return to traditional gender roles.

THE MORALITY MYTH: WOMEN REALLY WANT TO BE "PURE"!

Shalit's book received the most media attention by far; it was covered in dozens of articles, and she made a handful of television appearances. Much like her websites, Shalit's *Girls Gone Mild* asserts that girls really *want* to be modest and chaste, that they're naturally such, but that society and outside influences force them to be sexual. (In Shalit's worldview, women are naturally modest and chaste; if we're sexual at all, it's because of outside influences.) Her book argues that young women are rebelling against sexualized culture by forming a movement for chastity.

Shalit describes "Pure Fashion" shows as evidence of this modesty backlash. These events were started in 1999 by Catholic moms across the country who were sick of the skimpy clothing that was seemingly the only thing available for their daughters to wear. The shows, which feature clothing that cover more skin than most muumuus, would be a noble enough cause except for the etiquette classes they're paired with, better suited for girls growing up in the 1900s. The misleading purity rhetoric—that somehow it's "good" girls who wear these modest clothes and bad girls who don't—doesn't help, either. But most problematically (and untruthfully), Shalit describes the events as "mainstream," even though there were only seventeen held in 2006, hardly a high number for seven years of work.

As further evidence of the chastity movement, Shalit cites a boycott of the clothing company Abercrombie & Fitch by a group of high school girls, which was launched after the company produced shirts with messages such as WHO NEEDS BRAINS WHEN YOU HAVE THESE emblazoned across the breast area. Shalit fails to acknowledge that the boycott, which received national media attention, was in fact organized by a Pennsylvania-based *feminist* group, Girls as Grantmakers.[15] To attract support for her argument that this boycott demonstrated a commitment to "modesty" (as opposed to simply fighting sexism), she tries to distance the action from feminism, going so far as to write that one of the girls thought the National Organization for Women was "brainwashing." Shalit knew that Girls as Grantmakers was a feminist organization, but in order to fully appropriate the protest into her imagined modesty movement, she had to make it seem as if the girls involved were somehow opposed to feminism.*

Appropriating feminist language and action is nothing new in the conservative movement, but in Shalit's case it's particularly egregious, as she's attempting to create a "movement" out of thin air and shoddy reporting. She instead ought to be focusing on the national movement that does exist to fetishize virginity and modesty, and acknowledge that it's being led and energized by conservative institutions, not by young women—especially not young feminists who are working hard to battle sexist stereotypes, rather than promoting purity balls or modesty wear.

And while there's no question that American culture demands much of girls, including hypersexualization, there's no room in the virginity movement's analysis for the idea that young women may *want* to be sexy, to have sex, or to express themselves in ways that don't include wearing ankle-length skirts and finding husbands. The idea that young women could have a sexuality all their own is just too scary. And that's why Shalit's work speaks so acutely to parents and educators who are buying into the virginity movement's ideals. Shalit not only reinforces their beliefs about chastity and modesty, but also makes them believe that this limited vision of sexuality is something girls actually embrace.

It's no surprise, then, that Shalit's book—as well as most abstinence websites, for that matter—is peppered with quotes from 1940s teen advice guides and relies on good old-fashioned fear baiting. "The more experiences

---

* Girls as Grantmakers executive director Heather Arnet told me in a phone interview that she had agreed to let Shalit interview the teens (all minors) with her present. Shalit later contacted one of the girls without Arnet's or parental permission and engaged in long, leading email exchanges to get the exact quote she was looking for. Journalism at its finest!

teens have, the more likely they are to be depressed and commit suicide . . . this is particularly true of girls," Shalit writes.[16]

Similar ominous "statistics" are cited by Physicians for Life, whose website notes that "sexually active teens are more prone to be depressed/suicidal than teens who are chaste," and that "teenage girls who had sex were three times more likely to be depressed than girls who did not engage in sexual activity."[17]

No matter how revolutionary or forward-thinking Shalit might claim her ideas or the events she cites are, the virginity movement always returns to the idea that sex is dangerous for women, and that certain sexual choices (abstaining) are good, while others (not abstaining) are bad. Shalit even writes about "goodness" and "badness" explicitly in this way: "Conforming to badness is ultimately more oppressive than conforming to goodness."[18] "Empowering" rhetoric or not, there's nothing revolutionary about reinforcing the virgin/whore dichotomy.

THE EMOTIONAL/PHYSICAL MYTH: SEX MEANS SUFFERING

Stepp's *Unhooked* takes a more targeted look at girls "going wild," choosing to focus on the supposed decline of dating. Arguing that hookup culture has dangerous emotional consequences for young women, Stepp uses every trick in the backlash book to shame women for having premarital sex. She interviewed only a handful of young women—mostly white, upper class, and attending private school—over the course of a year.[19] During that time, some of the women hooked up and some were in more serious relationships, but instead of listening to the women she interviewed, Stepp pontificates about why they're not happy and what they should be doing. In a nutshell,

Stepp believes that premarital and casual sex aren't really what women want. Like Shalit, Stepp wants her readers to believe that what young women *really* want is to get married, have babies, and bake cookies.* Virginity Mommy knows best.

In a 2007 article for *The American Prospect,* deputy editor Ann Friedman (also a Feministing.com editor) wrote about how Stepp's theory is little more than regressive wishful thinking:

> She tells women they don't really like going out and getting drunk, they just think they do. ("Admit it, the bar scene is a guy thing.") . . . Stepp says women aren't naturally inclined to initiate sex. Back in the good old days "there were generally accepted rules back then about what to do and not do sexually," she wrote. "These standards restricted young women more than young men, by no means a fair deal, but they at least allowed women time and space to consider what kind of partners they wanted to love and what that love should look like." Because for Stepp, love, not academic or career ambitions, should be the focus of young women's energies.[20]

What Stepp recommends, quite literally, is for women to get out of the bar and back into the kitchen: "Guys will do anything for homemade baked goods," she writes. Somehow I can't get behind the idea that a generation of young women would give up casual sex for casual baking because a retrograde reporter promises it will be *so* much more fulfilling.

It's not all that surprising, however, that Stepp advocates a return to traditional gender roles. In 2006, she penned a piece for *The Washington Post* about how sexually aggressive girls (defined as those who don't mind initiating sexual

---

* Yes, cookies.

encounters) were responsible for a nationwide scourge of impotence.[21] Stepp seems to think that the future of erections everywhere are dependent on female subservience, so it's no wonder she's arguing so fervently for it!

A similar screed, *Unprotected,* which received the most coverage in Christian media, relies primarily on Grossman's experience as a campus psychiatrist at UCLA for its analysis. She argues that young women are not only increasingly more depressed because of hooking up, but also more diseased— physically *and* mentally. To drive home the fear her book is meant to incite, its cover shows a large picture of a young woman in a party dress and fishnet stockings sitting on the floor, slumped over, and seemingly passed out.*

Grossman blames what she calls politically correct campuses for not teaching young women that hookup culture can lead to sexually transmitted diseases. In a column published after *Unprotected* was released, she wrote:

> *For a teenage girl in 2008, "exploring" her sexuality places her at risk for some two dozen different bacteria, viruses, parasites, and fungi. She is likely to be infected soon after her sexual debut. This is due to the prevalence of these organisms, their ability to infect without symptoms, the widespread practice of casual sex with multiple "partners," the inconsistent and improper use of condoms, and to a girl's physiological vulnerability.[22]*

Grossman also touts bringing back dating and long-term relationships, as if they've disappeared entirely from public life. (I hate to be the one to tell Grossman this, but even if he buys you flowers and takes you out to dinner first, you can still get HPV.)

---

* Because the only kind of sex young women have is drunken post-party, regrettable sex, obviously.

The real danger in Grossman's sensationalized ideas about the dangers of sex, however, is the way the media perpetuates them. Syndicated conservative columnist Kathleen Parker, for example, wrote a glowing article in *The Washington Post* about Grossman's research on college campuses, going as far as to write that hooking up has "created a mental health crisis."[23] Parker also presented some very questionable claims that rely on Grossman's politicized version of science.

> *"The consequences are worse for young women," says Grossman. In her psychiatric practice, she has come to believe that women suffer more from sexual hook-ups than men do and wonders whether the hormone oxytocin is a factor. Oxytocin is released during childbirth and nursing to stimulate milk production and promote maternal attachment. It is also released during sexual activity for both men and women, hence the nickname "love potion."[24]*

Ah, oxytocin—it's the magical love drug that virginity-movement regulars cite as the reason young women should wait until marriage for sex. Oxytocin first became famous in the reproductive rights world when Eric Keroack, an abstinence-only proponent the Bush administration appointed to oversee reproductive health funding, claimed that women "who have misused their sexual faculty and become bonded to multiple persons will diminish the power of oxytocin to maintain a permanent bond with an individual." The short version? Too much sex equals no more love. (In keeping with the sex-as-dirty theme, it's worth noting that before Keroack resigned, he also said that "pre-marital sex is really modern germ warfare" and "sexual activity is a war zone."[25])

THE RELIGIOUS/POLITICAL MYTH:
SEX HAS LARGER-THAN-LIFE CONSEQUENCES

Women are used to hearing about how having premarital or "casual" sex will harm them. Liebau's *Prude* takes the argument a bit further, theorizing that young women's sexual activity is not only harmful to them, but also detrimental to society as a whole. Liebau writes that the United States "pays a heavy price" for young women's sexuality, and rattles off statistics about the national costs of treating STIs and welfare programs for young mothers. Liebau joins in on the health- and moral-scare fun, too. She writes that having sex "often condemns young women to a life of poverty and deprivation."[26] Once again, she offers very little in the way of real analysis, but provides a lot of salacious anecdotes to get readers' outrage antenna going, like listing all the various places in schools and communities where young people have been caught having sex.

Dawn Eden, who is also a well-known pro-life blogger at the Dawn Patrol,[27] uses her own life as a former rock critic and sexually active young woman in New York City to make her argument that chastity is best.

Eden writes that she spent much of her youth sleeping around in the hope that a man would want a more serious relationship, and that made her miserable. The problem here is that Eden assumes that all women who have sex outside of the confines of a serious relationship (specifically, marriage) are miserable as well.

She even goes so far as to write that women who have premarital sex aren't fully women: "[O]nly through chastity can all the graces that are part of being a woman come to full flower in you." Additionally, Eden seems to be convinced of the idea that women are inherently less-than. In a 2007 article for the *Times* (U.K.), Eden writes that women are "vessels [who] seek to be filled."[28] This sentiment is expressed rather unsubtly throughout much of Eden's book, reverberates throughout the virginity movement as a whole, and is what gives away the movement's true agenda: women's supposed inferiority and its link to our sexuality.

Outside of pathologizing female sexuality, there's another stark similarity between this spate of recent books and most literature on chastity and virginity: Lesbian women don't exist, nor does sex for pleasure. These two issues are highly connected in their absence from the virginity movement's conversations, because they speak to the same issue: Sex is okay only when it's happening with your husband. Therefore, women who are having lesbian sex and women who are engaging in sex for the pleasure of it simply don't register. After all, why even acknowledge sexuality that has nothing to do with traditional gender roles? It's not part of their goals for women, so they simply don't exist.

FOE, THY NAME IS FEMINISM

All of the above-mentioned authors, along with much of the media covering these imagined girls going wild, have arrived at similar conclusions about what cultural culprit is to blame for all of this sexuality gone wild: feminism.

In the eyes of the virginity movement, feminism promotes the idea that women should be exactly like men. Apparently, this includes being subject to the testosterone-driven sex craziness that supposedly is male desire. Thus, feminism is named in every book as one of the causes, if not the central cause, of the decline of women's sexual morality.

Prude author Liebau, who believes that premarital sex has widespread political consequences, has written, "Rather than themselves urging girls not to behave in ways that conform to the 'bad boy' stereotype (and which, objectively, are destructive), feminists instead label those who do so as enemies of female liberation."[29] (Claiming that feminists want to end "femininity" is a common antifeminist trope and an effective scare tactic. Never mind that the femininity antifeminists are so quick to defend often centers on subservience and regression.) Liebau has also written that feminism is "completely irrelevant and silly to most well-adjusted women."[30]

Eden has noted on her blog that the feminist movement is "inextricably linked with the movement for a sexual 'freedom' that was in fact 'utilitarianism'—a 'freedom without responsibilities' that is, as John Paul II said in his 'Letter to Families,' 'the opposite of love.'" And, of course, there's Stepp's above-mentioned epic article "Cupid's Broken Arrow," about feminism as the root of impotence.

The antifeminism connection isn't limited to the written word, though. These authors also have ties to virulently antifeminist organizations that are central to the virginity movement. Grossman, for example, is a senior fellow with the Clare Boothe Luce Policy Institute, a conservative women's organization that runs campaigns like "Bring back the hope chest"; Liebau is a regular columnist for the conservative, antifeminist publication *Townhall*; Stepp, Shalit, and Eden even spoke together at panel called "Modest Proposals" sponsored by antifeminist organizations.[31]

If the virginity movement cared about young women, the link to antifeminism wouldn't be so evident. What other movement has ensured that young women have the rights that they have today? Feminism is responsible not only for the decline in violence against women over the last decade, but also for equal pay and rights legislation, reproductive justice, and the list goes on. So I'm more than a little suspicious of those who see women's advancement as a *bad* thing. Besides, the regressive messages the virginity movement pushes through these books and the media is clue enough about what it really wants from women: not independence and adulthood, but submissiveness, "modesty," and adherence to traditional gender roles. Focusing on our sexuality is just one piece, and a tool, of the larger agenda. After all, there's a reason why the assumed goal for women in virginity-movement screeds is marriage and motherhood only: The movement believes that's the only thing women are meant for.

SEXUALITY REALITY

Despite these panicked myths and sensationalized media about the physical and emotional consequences of premarital sex and hooking up, the truth about young women's sexuality is far from scandalous—or even dangerous.

Nearly all Americans have premarital sex. In fact, by the age of forty-four, 99 percent of Americans will have had sex, and 95 percent of us will have had sex before marriage.[32]

Single women, the primary target of the virginity movement, are not excluded from these numbers. One-third of U.S. women, ages twenty to forty-four, are single, and nine out of ten of them have had sex.[33] The only thing that's really changed in recent years—despite the protestations of those who fondly reminisce about the good old days when women were pure—is that the median age of women's first marriage rose from 22 to 25.3. (I wonder how the numbers would change if same-sex marriage were recognized.)

Laura Lindberg, who conducted a study of single American women in 2008, said, "For the majority of adult women, living without a partner does not mean living without sex. Yet policymakers continue to promote policies that fly in the face of reality. By neglecting to teach our youth how to protect themselves against unwanted pregnancy and sexually transmitted diseases, we leave them ill prepared to become sexually healthy adults."[34]

Teens, too, are having sex—and a lot more responsibly than we give them credit for. They're using contraception more than ever, and teen pregnancy rates have been steadily dropping since the early 1990s, thanks to increased contraceptive use.[35] (Of course, abstinence proponents have tried to take credit for this decline, failing to note that the decrease in teen pregnancy preceded funding for abstinence-only education.[36])

That's not to say all is well, though. One-third of young American women get pregnant before they're twenty; of those who carry the pregnancy to term, 80 percent of the births are unintended.[37] And a 2008 study by the Centers for Disease Control and Prevention reported that one in four young women in the United States has a sexually transmitted infection.[38] Since this is the type of information the mainstream media loves to dwell on, these statistics have received an overwhelming amount of attention, most of it more panicked than necessary. The majority of those infections are HPV, most strains of which clear up on their own; the other infections were, likewise, on the less dangerous end of the STI scale.

Jacob Goldstein, of *The Wall Street Journal,* wrote in response to the study, "Indeed, several common infections lumped into the big bin labeled 'STD' can have mild or no effects on many patients—an issue that has prompted some leaders in the field to call for a dialing back of the nomenclature."[39] Perhaps there's less need for panic than we thought. So, without discounting the real harm of serious, and especially life-threatening, STIs, it's worth noting that the panic surrounding the escalating rates of infection might be a bit overblown.

What *is* cause for concern, however, is the racial and economic disparity in those numbers. Forty-eight percent of African American girls, ages fourteen to nineteen, for example, have had a sexually transmitted infection, compared with 20 percent of white teen girls.[40] STIs are disproportionately higher in low-income neighborhoods.[41] Yet, ironically, it's *these* young women whom the virginity movement forgets about—or ignores.

It's also difficult to take the virginity movement's concern about sexual health seriously when, arguably, the increase in STIs is a result not of casual sex, but instead of the predictable outcome of teaching a generation of young people that contraception doesn't work.

And regarding the claim that hookup culture is running rampant across America, it's simply not true—at least, not to the extent that extremists would have you believe it is. Young women are still forming short- and long-term relationships, and they're still dating, getting married, and having children. Just because they feel less stigmatized doesn't mean that they're out having sex willy-nilly. It's just another figment of the virginity movement's very active (and sexually obsessed) imagination. It's telling Americans what they want to hear—salacious stories about young girls having lots and lots of sex—under the rhetoric of helping women.

After all, what better way to sexify your cause than to focus it on virginity, promiscuity, and young girls' sexuality? By colluding with the cultural obsession over young women's sexuality, the virginity movement not only gets extra attention from the mainstream, it also ties women's sexuality with its larger agenda—to roll back *all* women's rights.

CHAPTER 3

forever young

"Virgins are hot."

T - S H I R T   S L O G A N ,
Heritage Community Services,
an abstinence-only organization

Six-year-olds don't need bras. In fact, you'd be hard pressed to find a girl under ten who requires one—even a training bra would be gratuitous. So when the nationwide superstore Target started selling Bratz* "bralettes"—padded (yes, *padded*) bras with cartoon characters on them marketed to girls—consumers and parents were justifiably horrified.[1] A similar reaction erupted when it was revealed that Wal-Mart was selling panties in its juniors' section with WHO NEEDS CREDIT CARDS . . . emblazoned across the front.[2]

Unfortunately, inappropriateness surrounding girls' sexuality doesn't end

---

* Bratz dolls are frequently cited when discussing girls' sexualization—the toys are dressed up in miniskirts, halter tops, and heavy makeup, sparking some people to say they look like "toy prostitutes."

with tacky underwear. Toy stores are selling plastic stripper poles, and "modeling" websites are featuring prepubescent girls posing in lingerie. Even mainstream pornography has caught on: In 2006, *Playboy* listed *Lolita,* Vladimir Nabokov's novel about a pedophile who falls in lust with his landlady's twelve-year-old daughter, as one of the "25 Sexiest Novels Ever Written."[3] I love Nabokov and I thought *Lolita* was brilliant. But sexy? Seducing a twelve-year-old?

The message is clear, and dangerous: The most desirable women aren't women at all—they're *girls.*

But this isn't news. Most of us are aware of how subject girls are to inappropriate sexual attention, and how younger and younger women are presented as sex objects in the media. What *is* news, though, is how this sexualization is coming from someplace other than an easy-to-blame hypersexualized pop culture—it's also coming from the virginity movement.

After all, the "perfect virgin" is at the center of the movement's rhetoric, and its goals revolve largely around convincing girls that the only way to be pure is to abstain from sex. This means there's an awful lot of talk about young girls' sexuality in the movement, from T-shirts like the one quoted above to abstinence classes to purity balls. By focusing on the virginity of young women and girls, the movement is doing exactly what it purports to abhor—objectifying women and reducing them to their sexuality.

And while there has been public outrage over girls' sexualization—when it comes to bralettes at Target or the ways in which girls are portrayed in ads, for example—much of this concern focuses on what affects our "perfect virgins," not on the more insidious sexualization coming from the virginity movement, or the kind that hurts girls whom the media doesn't care about.

Case in point: Bratz dolls, provocative Halloween costumes, and panty-less pop singers dominate public discourse and outrage, while even more obvious (and, arguably, more dangerous) sexualization of girls—like trafficking, rape, and child pornography—isn't given nearly the same amount of attention. It's no coincidence that these more serious issues are ones that overwhelmingly affect low-income girls, girls of color, and young women who don't match the American virginal ideal.*

And, sadly, it's not just girls who are bearing the brunt of what author M. Gigi Durham calls the "Lolita effect."[4] Grown women, buying into the notion that the only desirable sexuality is a young one, are embracing girlishness in more and more ways—even getting plastic surgery on their genitals just to be seen as sexually attractive and youthful.

But whether it's training girls to be women before their time or expecting women to act and look like little girls, when youth is the most desirable sexual characteristic and girls are the most desirable sexual beings, all of us suffer.

PURE GIRLS

There's no doubt that the sexualization of girls has hit a crisis point. You need look no further than something as simple as Halloween—long gone are the days of girls dressing up as ghosts, witches, or a beloved superhero. Now the standard costume is "sexy ghost" or "*Playboy* witch."† (There are even child "pimp" and "ho" costumes.) But we don't sexify girls just one day a year; you

---

* I'm not arguing that we should be paying more attention to one kind of sexualization than to another, but there's a disturbing gap when it comes to *which* girls we're more apt to hear about.

† Yes, these exist. I'm somewhat embarrassed to admit that as a freshman in college (at Tulane University in New Orleans), I succumbed to the sexy-costume craze by donning a white minidress with a red cross drawn across the chest—I was a "nurse." I promptly learned my lesson after a male passerby on Bourbon Street screamed out that I was a "bloody-hot nurse." I thought perhaps he was British, but alas, he was actually oh-so-subtly letting me know that I had gotten my period early that month.

can buy your daughter a *Playboy* pencil set or your infant Heelicious shoes—baby stilettos—anytime!

"There has been a marked shift in the proliferation of hypersexualized imagery being marketed to younger and younger girls, as well as more representations of very young girls—I'm talking about tweens and preschoolers—in sexually provocative poses and contexts," says Durham, author of *The Lolita Effect: The Media Sexualization of Young Girls and What We Can Do About It.*[5] "These are highly repressive and regressive notions of sexuality, not healthy, accurate, or developmentally appropriate concepts of sex."

A 2007 report from the American Psychological Association (APA) found that nearly *every form* of media studied provided "ample evidence of the sexualization of women," and that most sexualization focused on young women.[6]* The report also showed that this sexualization did not come from media alone. Girls' relationships with parents, educators, and peers further contributed to the problem.

> [P]arents may convey the message that maintaining an attractive physical appearance is the most important goal for girls. Some may allow or encourage plastic surgery to help girls meet that goal. Research shows that teachers sometimes encourage girls to play at being sexualized adult women or hold beliefs that girls of color are "hypersexual" and thus unlikely to achieve academic success. Both male and female peers have been

---

* The APA defines sexualization as when "a person's value comes only from his or her sexual appeal or behavior, to the exclusion of other characteristics; a person is held to a standard that equates physical attractiveness (narrowly defined) with being sexy; a person is sexually objectified—that is, made into a thing for others' sexual use, rather than seen as a person with the capacity for independent action and decision making; and/or sexuality is inappropriately imposed upon a person."

found to contribute to the sexualization of girls—girls by policing each
other to ensure conformance with standards of thinness and sexiness and
boys by sexually objectifying and harassing girls.[7]

Girls are getting it from all angles—home, school, and the media. What makes matters worse, according to Durham, is that the girls being targeted are even younger than they were in years past. The reason behind it? "It may be a backlash against the fact that women are succeeding in life in ways they never did before, and little girls represent a traditional version of docile, passive femininity," says Durham.*

Touting girls and girlhood as ideal forms of sexuality is simply another way of advancing the notion that to be desirable, women need to be un-adults—young, naive, and impressionable. Being independent, assured, and grown up has no place in this disconcerting model.

The virginity movement is fighting sexualization with *more* sexualization—we just don't always recognize it as such because it's shrouded in language about modesty, purity, and protection.

Take the latest trend in virginity worship: purity balls. Fathers escort their daughters to these promlike balls, where at some point—between the dancing, food, and entertainment (largely involving little girls doing ballet around big wooden crosses)—the girls recite a pledge vowing to be chaste until marriage, and name their fathers as the "keepers" of their virginity until a husband takes their place. Sounds a bit old school, but these events are becoming a nationwide

---

* Ah, the ethics of passivity rears its ugly head! Not only do women need to do nothing (remain sexually abstinent) in order to be moral, we also must remain inert if we want to be considered sexy.

phenomenon and receiving widespread media attention—from *The New York Times* to *Dr. Phil*—and parties are being planned in nearly every state in America.

Pastor Randy Wilson and his wife, Lisa, founded purity balls in 1998 in Colorado Springs.[8] The Wilsons, who have seven children (five of them daughters), write in a letter to purity ball planners that they founded the balls because they saw that "the protection of the daughter's purity rested on the shoulders of the fathers" and they wanted to create an event that conveyed that sentiment.

This "protection" is articulated in a pledge that fathers recite, promising to "cover" their daughters and protect their purity:

> I, [daughter's name]'s father, choose before God to cover my daughter as her authority and protection in the area of purity. I will be pure in my own life as a man, husband, and father. I will be a man of integrity and accountability as I lead, guide, and pray over my daughter and as the high priest in my home. This covering will be used by God to influence generations to come.[9]*

It's hard to know what's more problematic: the pseudo-incestuous talk of covering or the antiquated notion that fathers own their daughters and their sexuality. Perhaps the upside of these balls, however, is how overtly they epitomize the ideals of the virginity movement. There's no hiding behind the rhetoric of empowerment here—the message is clear and direct: It's up to men to control young women's sexuality. (In fact, that message is furthered in newer

---

* I was horrified (but not surprised) when, after I repeated this pledge at a talk I was giving at Cornell University in 2008, a student shouted out that "covering" is a term used to describe breeding horses. One horse "covers" another.

events sponsored for young men and their mothers: integrity balls.* Instead of pledging their virginities to their mothers, however, the young men and boys in this ball vow not to sully someone's daughter or future wife. So, in either event, maintaining women's purity—and men's ownership—is the goal!)

And though the idea behind the pledge and ball is to promote purity, the symbolism is far from chaste. In one online video of a purity ball, the girls recite the virginity pledge as they give little pink boxes (ahem) to their fathers.[11] Some fathers participating in purity balls give their daughter a charm necklace with a lock and key. The daughter keeps the lock and her father holds on to the key until she gets married and he gives the "key" to her husband.[12]†

Also troubling is that the event is described as a "date." The girls—some as young as six or seven—dress in ball gowns and often get their hair and makeup professionally done. In a *Glamour* magazine article about purity balls, reporter and noted feminist Jennifer Baumgardner wrote that many of the older girls in attendance look "disconcertingly like wives" next to their fathers.[13] In a way, that's the point: Young women are being trained to be not autonomous adults, but perpetual children whose sexuality is strictly defined and owned, like that of traditional wives-in-training.#

The conservative Christian organization Focus on the Family, for example, encourages fathers to take their daughters on "date nights" in order to

---

* As my coblogger Ann Friedman put it: "Why is this glamorous evening not called a purity ball, too? Because it's not up to young men to stay "pure." They just have to seek out a wife who is."[10]

† Subtlety is a bit lost on the virginity movement, especially when it comes to any kind of phallic symbol.

When I first came across purity balls, I wondered if my feminism had jaded me *too* much. Maybe these were just daddy/daughter dances that I was imbuing with sexual meaning. So I showed my father some video footage of a purity ball and asked what he thought. The color drained from his face and he just said, "Jessica, that's truly fucking weird."

"affirm [their] femininity."* The promotional materials that describe these dates use language that one would think would make participants uneasy, but instead are positioned as sweet and doting:

> Katie giggles as she waits for her date to come around and open the car door. The pair enters an ice cream shop. She sits down at the table as her date gently pushes in her chair. He takes her hand from across the table and asks, "What flavor would you like tonight, Sugar?" Katie smiles and says, "I'll have chocolate, Daddy." More and more fathers are becoming aware of their influence and are regularly dating their daughters."[14]

Dating their daughters? Isn't it possible to encourage fathers to spend more time with their daughters without using language usually reserved for romantic relationships? Neutral, family-based rhetoric would probably be just as effective and would certainly be less, well, creepy. But calling daddy/daughter quality time "dates" speaks volumes about how young women are valued in the virginity movement—for their sexuality.

While I was researching purity balls, this quote from Wesley Tullis, who has taken both of his daughters to the events, really stuck with me: "It is impossible to convey what I have seen in their sweet spirits, their delicate, forming souls, as their daddy takes them out for their first, big dance. Their whole being absorbs my loving attention, resulting in a radiant sense of self-worth and identity."[15] There's no doubt that a loving relationship between father and daughter can be a wonderful thing. But just how healthy is it to conflate virginity with "self-worth" and "identity," and paternal attention with sexuality?

---

* In the world of the virginity movement, "femininity" is synonymous with submissiveness and girlishness.

In fact, it's difficult to watch videos of purity balls, or read the "dating your daughter" literature, and *not* think about these pseudo-incestuous themes—and whether they might be connected to real-life abuse.

In a piece in *The New York Times* on purity balls, Judith Warner notes that even if there is no crime in these events, "there is nonetheless a kind of horror to [fathers'] obsession with their daughters' sexuality":

> *Judith Lewis Herman, a clinical professor of psychiatry at Harvard Medical School, whose work with and writings on incest victims in the 1980s revolutionized the understanding of the crime and its perpetrators, believes that incest, like rape generally, has to be viewed within a wider context of power relations. Incest, she says, is "an abuse of patriarchal power," a criminal perversion of fatherly control and influence. It is perpetrated, in many cases, by men who present themselves as the guardians of the moral order.*[16]

The Wilsons, however, insist that purity balls and virginity pledges aren't about focusing on girls' sexuality. "Of course, we want to do everything we can to help them enter marriage as pure, as whole persons," Lisa said in a 2001 *Gazette* article. "But it's not just physical. It's moral and emotional purity."[17]

Yet again, the foundation of a girl's "moral and emotional purity" and her ability to be a "whole" person is boiled down to her being a virgin! While proponents of date nights and purity balls argue that they're aiming to protect girls from sexualization, by focusing on girls' virginity they're actually positioning girls as sexual objects before they've even hit puberty.*

---

* If you're thinking that the mysterious world of purity balls doesn't affect you and yours, and that the events are simply a creepy anomaly, remember that these virginity fetish free-for-alls are *federally funded.*

What's particularly ironic is that while the virginity movement denounces the sexualization of girls in mainstream culture, it fails to see how its own form of virginity worship is much the same thing.

When the outrage over the padded bras at Target hit the media, for example, a spokesperson from Bratz, the doll company that produces the bras, argued that the padding was for girls "to be discreet as they develop . . . it's more about hiding what you have got than showing it off. . . . [The bralettes] give girls modesty and style as they go through development changes." (When U.K. superstore Tesco was criticized for selling a different brand of padded bras for young girls, a spokesperson for the company said nearly the same thing: "It is a product designed for girls at that self-conscious age when they are just developing."[18])

The message *seems* contradictory—padded bras as a way to promote "modesty"? But, as with purity balls and our purity princesses put on pedestals for their abstinence, fetishizing virginity (and young girls) is explained away as simply exalting modesty and virtue.

A similar theme woven through both purity culture and pop culture is the valorizing of "innocence" in girls—simply a sly way of focusing on virginity yet again. This idea has been popping up in specific controversies, and it reeks of feigned concern.

When the FDA was considering making a cervical cancer vaccine available in the United States, for example, the single biggest public concern— even after it was deemed safe and legalized—wasn't health related or about the vaccine's newness. It was about "innocence"—specifically, the worry that girls would become promiscuous if they were vaccinated.

The cancer vaccine, now sold as Gardasil, prevents human papillomavirus (HPV), a sexually transmitted infection that causes cervical cancer.

Opponents of the vaccine—the usual suspects, such as conservative religious groups and antifeminist organizations—argued that girls would be more likely to have sex if they thought they were "safe."*

Charlotte Allen, of the antifeminist organization the Independent Women's Forum, wrote that the HPV vaccine gives girls the message that "it's just fine for them to have all the sex they want, 'cuz now they'll be vaccinated!"[19] Bridget Maher, of the Family Research Council, said that giving girls the vaccine is harmful because "they may see it as a license to engage in premarital sex."[20] Dozens of other conservative pundits and organizations repeated the sentiment. I rarely quote Bill Maher, but he was right on when he noted, "It's like saying if you give a kid a tetanus shot, she'll want to jab rusty nails in her feet."[21]

Then came the incessant chatter about innocence. In an interview with *The Washington Post,* one Pennsylvania pediatrician called the vaccine an "assault on [girls'] innocence."[22] In a post on Wendy Shalit's blog, Modestly Yours, Elizabeth Neville wrote about the vaccine in a post titled "Immunized Against Innocence?"; another organization opposing the vaccine took the subtle route, naming itself Parents Promoting Innocence.[23] Per usual, the virginity movement sought to protect an amorphous idea like "innocence" or "virginity," rather than taking strong, tangible action on behalf of girls' well-being. Where was the outrage over actual health concerns—you know, like *cancer?*

The innocence trope isn't limited to specific controversies, either. It seems the mere act of girls becoming women has the American public in a tizzy.

In a 2008 MSNBC medical article, for example, doctor/reporter Billy Goldberg bemoaned how girls are beginning to menstruate at younger and

---

* Virginity movement logic: Better that girls risk getting cancer than be sexually active.

younger ages. "What happened to the innocence of youth?" he asked. He also wrote, "Earlier onset of puberty is associated with health concerns beyond the loss of youthful innocence."[24]

If being premenstrual is "innocence," does that make those of us with periods *guilty?* And this really gets to the heart of the matter: These concerns aren't about lost innocence; they're about lost girlhood. *The virginity movement doesn't want women to be adults.*

Despite the movement's protestations about how this focus on innocence or preserving virginity is just a way of protecting girls, the truth is, it isn't a way to desexualize them. It simply positions their sexuality as "good"— worth talking about, protecting, and valuing—and women's sexuality, adult sexuality, as bad and wrong. The (perhaps) unintended consequence of this focus is that girls' sexuality is sexualized and fetishized even further.

With every virginity pledge taken and every girl sexualized in the media, what the virginity movement—and perhaps even American culture at large— wants for young women becomes clearer and clearer: perpetual girlhood.

GIRLIFYING WOMEN

Back in my teenage days in New York City, everyone wanted to go to raves, techno music–fueled dance parties where drugs were abundant.* Putting aside the dangers of teenage drinking and drug use for a moment, the girls' fashion of that time is worth some examination. I recall wearing baby barrettes in my hair (hey, it was the style!) and my friends carrying pacifiers around their necks. Unlike riot grrrls (the early-'90s punk feminists inspired by bands like Bikini Kill—who sometimes mimicked girlhood by wearing

---

* I know, the image of your feminist author dancing around with glowsticks doesn't exactly inspire confidence or gravitas, but it is what it is.

Hello Kitty or otherwise "young" clothing as a subversive statement about femininity), the rave fashion scene seemed much more about playing up little girls' sexuality. Mercifully, the trend waned, but similar fashions have popped up in its place: Schoolgirl-style knee socks paired with heels are popular right now in hipster sects, for example. But fashion is just one cultural indicator of the girlhood fetish—and probably the most innocuous. Over the last two decades, the valorizing of youth and youth culture has hit women particularly hard. Women want to be young—often at too high a cost.

Take vaginal rejuvenation,* the fastest-growing form of plastic surgery in the United States,[25] and probably the best example of how women are expected to be girls—and not just girls, but *virginal* girls. (After all, how much more obvious can the virginity fetish be when women are obtaining a surgery that makes their vaginas younger?)

The surgery, touted using feminist rhetoric—"Women now have equal sexuality rights!" says one press release—claims to give women's vaginas a "youthful aesthetic look."[26] Virgin vaginas, ready to order!

Rejuvenation, which costs anywhere from $2,000 to $5,000, can include a labia trim, liposuction on the outer lips, tightening the vaginal muscles, or a hymenoplasty (in which the doctor constructs a fake hymen). And although the risks are serious—infection, hemorrhaging, loss of sensitivity, scarring, nerve damage, painful intercourse, and disfigurement—women are lining up to get the surgery.

Why? Well, in addition to the "youthful aesthetic," many women seem to believe that their genitals simply aren't normal. The American College of Obstetricians and Gynecologists (ACOG) says that most women don't understand the size and shape of genitalia correctly, and that physicians performing vaginal

---

* As if a woman's vagina were simply exhausted before the surgery.

surgeries may be leading women to have "misguided assumptions" about what is normal.[27] The ACOG even went as far as to release a warning about the surgery, noting that it is "deceptive" for doctors to give patients the impression that these procedures are "accepted and routine surgical practices."[28]

But "normalcy" in this regard is hard to define, given our porned culture. The Vaginal Rejuvenation Institute, for example, says on its website that "many women bring us magazines such as *Playboy*" to show the doctor the aesthetic they're looking for. "Normalcy" is no longer defined by women—it's defined by porn magazines and movies that feature young girls and uniform-looking vulvae.

Psychologist and sex therapist Laurie Betito, speaking in Montreal in 2005 at the 17th World Congress of Sexology, said that "the pathologizing of changes associated with age creates a surgical esthetic," even when it comes to our vaginas. Women in America *already* pathologize aging, so it's no surprise that they'd be so keen to fall in line to alter the next body part we're meant to obsess over.

The real disservice to women here is that despite the fact that the plastic-surgery industry frames vaginal rejuvenation as "freeing" and benefiting women, the procedure's real purpose is rarely for women's pleasure—it's almost always done for either men's physical pleasure or aesthetic acceptance.* Most of the personal stories on surgeons' websites and in media coverage recall women's getting the surgery as a "gift" for their husbands or male partners.

Thirty-two-year-old Lisseth Figueroa of Los Angeles, for example, said in *The Washington Post* that she got the surgery to save her marriage. "I did it for both of us. . . . Before the surgery I felt really old . . . and ugly. Since the surgery, that's changed. I'm very happy with it—and so is my husband."[29]

---

* It occurs to me that when this surgery is performed on women in Africa, we call it female genital mutilation, but in the oh-so-enlightened United States, we call them designer vaginas. You know, because American women are *empowered.*

Another woman, on an online forum for women who have gotten or are considering the surgery, says she underwent a hymen replacement so that her husband could "take [her] virginity again." This goes to show just how silly the notion of virginity really is. After all, these women aren't *actually* becoming virgins, they're just getting the supposed physical characteristics thereof—and even that's questionable. As Hanne Blank points out in her book *Virgin,* the hymen is not really an indicator of virginity at all: "Hymens and vaginas vary considerably, as do reactions to vaginal penetration." In other words, there really isn't any way to tell if a woman has had sex. So why the hymen obsession?

> We became aware of hymens because we are aware of something we call virginity. We found the hymen because we found reasons to search women's bodies for some bit of flesh that embodied this quality we call "virginity," some physical proof that it existed.[30]

Interesting to consider, isn't it, that someone somewhere, at some point in history, decided to figure out a way to measure a woman's virginity—regardless of the fact that there are certainly other ways to break a hymen? It's no surprise, then, that hymenoplasty in particular is so intensely tied up with the purity myth: Despite the fact that a virginity/hymen connection is not absolute, women are desperate to have a physical indicator of virginity. That's how embedded the myth is in our psyches.

Unfortunately, trying to turn women into little girls doesn't stop at terrifying genital surgeries. Lest women be seen as too womanly, they can also get "mommy makeovers" right after they give birth. This postpartum plastic surgery gives new moms a tummy tuck, breast lift, and liposuction, all to get their younger, non-mom bodies back. Or there's also the MILF (mom I'd like to fuck) trend in pop and porn culture, in which "hot moms" are those who look more like college students than mothers. Or schoolgirl outfits for grown women (think Halloween or the popular girl "band" the Pussycat Dolls—those short plaid skirts are everywhere!). And, of course, there's the prevalence of virgin porn, in which young-looking actresses pretend to lose their virginity (generally to much older men). The valorization of youth, and especially of virginity, is everywhere.

But for some women, young or old, plastic surgeries and Bratz bralettes are the least of their worries. Too many women struggle just to be seen.

INVISIBLE GIRLS

Certain kinds of sexualization, terrifying kinds, affect girls daily and yet rarely make the news or appear on the virginity movement's radar. When it comes to girls who are trafficked or forced into the sex trade, there's relatively little outrage or talk about "lost innocence." Perhaps that's because these girls weren't considered innocent in the first place.

Approximately two hundred thousand to three hundred thousand adolescents are sexually exploited—through prostitution, trafficking, child sex tourism, or pornography—annually in the United States.[31] According to Rachel Lloyd,* founder and executive director of Girls Educational & Men-

---

* Lloyd's own story is worth telling: When she was thirteen years old, she left school to take care of her alcoholic mother. After working in factories and restaurants in her home country of England, she quickly turned to criminal activity as a way to make money. It wasn't long before she got heavily involved in drugs and relationships with older men. By age seventeen, Lloyd had moved to Germany and was turning tricks in a Munich strip club. It wasn't until her pimp tried to kill her that she turned to a local church for help. Years later, in 1999, she founded GEMS, which provides preventative and transitional services to young, mostly teenage women who are involved in prostitution or sexually violent situations.[32]

toring Services (GEMS) in New York City, many of the girls who are being exploited and have no place to go for help are often overlooked because they don't qualify as "perfect virgins."

In a report on how to best advocate for girls who are sexually exploited and trafficked for money, Lloyd notes that in areas like New York City, such victims are often young women of color from low-income communities "who are perceived as inherently 'loose,' unredeemable, and hopeless."

"These young women are often not just absent from public debate, but actively denigrated and seen as complicit in their abuse," Lloyd writes.[33]

Instead of receiving help, these girls are often persecuted—they're arrested and punished by a system that sees them not as victims, but as criminals.

Ironically, if the girls Lloyd helps were smuggled in from China or trafficked from some eastern European country, rather than having grown up in the Bronx, they'd be given federal protection under the Trafficking Victims Protection Act. But in New York, the girls Lloyd works with are considered prostitutes—criminals who should be locked up no matter how young they are or how dire the circumstances they come from might be. And because they are overwhelmingly young, low-income women of color, the system is all too happy to oblige. Try to imagine a scourge of blonde teen girls being arrested and thrown in juvenile detention after being raped, abused, and forced to sell their bodies—people would be marching in the street; the media would be outraged. But for the girls of GEMS, there's only silence.

Unfortunately, exploitation doesn't stop on the streets. With the advent of the Internet, more insidious forms of sexualization are broadcast for the world to see—yet remain on the margins of the public's radar. As authorities crack down on child pornography online, pedophiles are finding new and improved ways to circumvent the law; the latest is child "supermodel" websites.

Featuring pictures of prepubescent girls posing provocatively in bikinis, underwear (often thongs), or clothing that is, at best, disturbingly inappropriate, these websites promote themselves as child "modeling" sites, though they're clearly marketed toward a predatory audience.

Julie Posey of Pedowatch, an online watchdog group aimed at protecting children, recently said in *Wired* magazine, "Why else would someone pay to see kids in their underwear?"[34]

When *Wired* investigated these websites—which are owned primarily by one company based in Florida—the virtual fan club members' comments made the sites' intentions crystal clear:

> *[There are] men with nicknames such as "Cum ta Poppa." At one of Amber's fan clubs, "humberthaze" writes: "We only get glimpses of her potential when she does a bit of 'bump and g,' but then she quickly relapses into something awkward and childish. Sometimes you can hear the photographer get excited when she gives us what we/he want(s). She'll do a little killer wiggle and we hear him say quickly, 'What was that?' or 'Do that again!!!'"*

One user even complained, "She's gotten too developed for my taste, I doubt I'll be an Amber fan anymore."

It doesn't get much more obvious than that, but because these websites don't show children engaging in real or simulated sex, they're legal.

Obviously, websites like these, unlike purity balls or padded bras, are *overtly* sexual. But the line is surprisingly thin. Think about it: How different is deliberately turning young girls into sex objects by having them pose in underwear from getting them dolled up for a child beauty pageant or a date with Daddy? Yes, the former is meant to elicit sexual arousal, but just because the latter is couched in the language of purity doesn't make it any less sexual. Either way, the focus is still on girls' sexuality, and it's still making them "women" before their time.

OUR HYMENS, OURSELVES?

Whether it's surgery or purity balls, a woman dressing up like a Catholic schoolgirl for Halloween or a child dressing in a ball gown for a beauty pageant, the common theme is that women's—nay, *girls'*—sexuality has become our only truly valued personal characteristic. And for America's invisible girls, that fetishization often means a life of violence and punishment (more on the way women are punished for violating purity guidelines in Chapter 7).

Any way you slice it, women's identities are so tied up with whether or not we've had sex, or how sexual or abstinent we are, that it's become almost impossible to think of ourselves as women outside of that framework. And really, while it's pop culture that gets the most attention in this regard, it's the virginity movement that's reinforcing the notion.

After all, what's the difference, *really,* between the shirt sold at purity balls—a tight babydoll tee that says, I'M WAITING—and the one recently pulled from Delia's (a clothing store for preteen and teenage girls) that shouts in rainbow colors, I'M TIGHT LIKE SPANDEX? Sure, the Delia's tee is the more vulgar of the two, but the intent is the same. They both announce virginity and they both make clear that virginity—or at least its assumed physical attributes—is a part of the wearer's identity.

In my interview with Durham, she noted that "girls need information, support and nurture as they move into a sexually empowered adulthood where they can make intelligent and intentional sexual choices for themselves." That's what we need to be fighting for—a nuanced, respectful, informed vision of sexuality for young girls. Because what we have now—sexualization and fetishization—is hurting girls every day.

the porn connection

"It is commonly believed that mainstream
pornography is represented by the centerfolds
in today's men's magazines. In fact, that is precisely
what the ACLU and the sex industry want us
to think. But if a man were to go into the sex shops
on Times Square or in other large cities in the
United States, he would find very few depictions of
normal heterosexual activity. Instead, he would see
a heavy emphasis on violent homosexual
and lesbian scenes. . . . Amazingly, there is a huge
market for disgusting materials of this nature."
FOCUS ON THE FAMILY[1]

ON MTV'S SHOW *I Want a Famous Face,* nineteen-year-old Sha told the
camera that she wanted to look like Pamela Anderson so she could pursue a
career as a *Playboy* model. During the show, viewers watched as Sha underwent surgery to get breast implants, lip implants, and liposuction on her
chin—all so she could have that *Playboy* look. Sadly, Sha's story is a dime
a dozen; the mainstreaming of pornography is influencing young women
across the country. Pornish pubic hair (or lack thereof) is inspiring a generation of women to take it all off. Porn star Jenna Jameson's book, *How to
Make Love Like a Porn Star: A Cautionary Tale,* spent six weeks on *The New*

York Times bestseller list. There's even a reality television show on E! that follows the lives of Hugh Hefner's *Playboy* Bunny girlfriends.

There is little doubt that pornography is pervasive in America—from Internet porn to PORN STAR shirts for preteens, we're simply inundated with it. But while this "porning of America"* is vastly more present than the virginity movement and its cultural output, the latter actually relies on the former for its survival. You can't have purity without perceived impurity, after all. The virginity movement's success—its ability to appear relevant, even—depends on its having a social evil to rail against. Movement leaders *need* pornography in order to justify the extreme nature of the purity message they're pushing. Pornography and purity may make strange bedfellows, but they're sharing sheet space all the same.

Naturally, porn culture raises serious questions and concerns about the oversexualization of women and girls (as discussed in Chapter 3) and the societal effects of pornography's being so readily accessible and so much more hardcore than past porn. But the virginity movement is using what could be a progressive conversation about women, men, and sexuality to carelessly push a regressive agenda. Instead of focusing the discourse on porn itself, the movement simply declares that *everything* is pornographic—teen clothing styles, books, television shows, even teaching students about birth control. You name it, it's pornographic and inappropriate. By taking on porn in this narrow way, the virginity movement's answers are similarly simplistic: Stop having sex. Stop porn. Be pure.†

By further promoting the virgin/whore dichotomy, the movement also

---

* As it was referred to by Carmine Sarracino and Kevin Scott in their book, *The Porning of America.*

† And send our organizations money to fight the good fight against obscenity!

inadvertently ensures that young women *will* engage in porn culture—be it through *Playboy* pencil cases,* Girls Gone Wild, or simply thinking that porn is "cool." By erasing any nuance and complexity from conversations about porn and sexuality, the virginity movement gives young women only two choices of who they can be sexually: sluts or not sluts. While the first choice doesn't seem attractive, I can guarantee you that most young women are going to go with the option that allows them to have sex. And there's no in-between identity for young women who are making smart, healthy choices in their sexual lives.

Most important (as evidenced by the quote starting off this chapter), the issues the virginity movement is concerned with *aren't* those that have to do with helping women. They don't care about sex workers' rights or the objectification and dehumanization of women that some porn peddles in. They care about maintaining the sexual status quo: Men are men, women are subservient and chaste, and sexuality is shameful.

A PORNED AMERICA

When I was in college, my then-boyfriend Mike told me how he first encountered pornography. His parents got the Playboy TV channel on cable, and because he had a television in his room, it wasn't long before he discovered the joys of softcore clips and montages of naked women. Today, a teen boy will more likely come across "2 girls, 1 cup"† than find his parents' dirty-magazine stash. To put it mildly, pornography is not what it used to be.

While the porn film *Deep Throat*—which was released in 1972 and

---

* Yes, these exist.

† A porn clip that became an Internet phenomenon, "2 girls, 1 cup" features two women defecating into a cup, eating the excrement, and throwing up into each other's mouths.

received accolades from reputable media, like *The New York Times*—is often credited as the beginning of the mainstreaming of pornography, Sarracino and Scott write that it was *Playboy* magazine, founded in 1953, that really changed the culture. Before that, porn was cheaply made, illicit, underground, and seedy, but with its quality publishing style, *Playboy* marked a shift in the way Americans viewed pornography.

> *Shame—the shame of poverty, transgression, the shame of the outsider— was in a sense encoded into the early presentations of pornography. Shame inhibits identification. We don't want to see as "ourselves" those who are socially, morally, and legally stigmatized. . . . In the case of* Playboy, *readers hefted the slick pages of stunning photographs of wholesome, beautiful girls, intermixed with images of and information about high-end stereo equipment, hip apartments, and sports cars, and thought, consciously or not:* This is me! This is who I am—or who I want to be![2]

Deep Throat, the plot of which revolved around a woman who discovers her clitoris is in her throat,* had a similar effect in the '70s. Instead of following the typical stag-film format, *Deep Throat* ran the length of a normal movie, featured a script with characters and a plot, and had a starring actress—Linda Lovelace. Celebrities admitted to loving the film, and it's still the highest-grossing porn of all time.

But it was in-home pornography—the advent of videotaped pornography and the Internet—that created the porn that we know today: increasingly hardcore, mainstream, and ubiquitous.[3] Today, estimated annual

---

* No nuance about male fantasy here!

porn sales in the United States are $10 billion;[4]* in fact, the U.S. revenue from Internet porn alone was $2.84 billion in 2006.[5] Of the approximately 372 million pornographic web pages worldwide, 89 percent are produced within the United States.

Because personal technology—be it a video camera, webcam, or blog—is readily available to most Americans, almost anyone can produce porn in the comfort of their own home. This ease of both making and consuming pornography has exponentially increased the amount of porn that's created, as well as the acceptability of pornography as part of American culture. (Thankfully, this democratization of porn has also meant an increase in feminist- and woman-friendly pornography—more on this later.)

There is no doubt that mainstream† pornography, like most pop culture, is problematic when it comes to the way women are represented and treated. As Robert Jensen wrote in *Getting Off: Pornography and the End of Masculinity,* "Pornography as a mirror shows us how men see women. Not all men, of course—but the ways in which many men who accept the conventional conception of masculinity see women. It's unsettling to look in that mirror."[6]

Jensen argues that while mainstream pornography in all forms tends to be misogynistic, it's reality, or "gonzo," porn—in which the sex workers acknowledge the camera's presence—that is most disturbing.

---

* Porn revenue numbers are often contested because it's difficult to know how much money is coming in from porn websites, but I'd argue anything in the billions equals pretty damn mainstream.
† When I write about mainstream porn, I'm referring to the bulk of the commercial porn industry—not including feminist and pro-woman porn, which, unfortunately, is not nearly as prevalent.

In gonzo, those same [sexual] acts are featured but typically are per-
formed in rougher fashion, often with more than one man involved, and
with more explicitly denigrating language that marks women as sluts,
whores, cunts, nasty bitches, and so on.[7]

It's hard to argue with Jensen's contention that the majority of gonzo pornography is made with women's debasement in mind. It's what Shauna Swartz called "humilitainment" in a 2004 *Bitch* magazine article; it's the kind of porn that revels in coaxing or "tricking" women into having sex, just to spit or ejaculate in their face at the end (as is the case with the popular website BangBus.com, where women are dumped by the side of the road and stranded after they've had sex).

"Tagging these disturbing spectacles of deception and abuse with the 'reality' label enhances their allure, as it claims to offer consumers unstaged and authentic action," wrote Swartz.[8]*

Naturally, not all porn humiliates women—there's a strong feminist porn culture, and mainstream porn that isn't misogynistic does exist. But in an industry that is constantly looking for the next, biggest, most extreme thing (gang bangs where hundreds of men line up to have sex with one woman, and the stomach-churning "2 girls, 1 cup," come to mind) it's near impossible to argue that porn culture isn't affecting American society detrimentally.

---

* The idea that someone would want to consume "authentically" humiliating films is discouraging, to say the least, but it parallels current cultural notions of American women as stupid and vapid.

There are many (many, many) genres of pornography, but what I find most interesting is the kind of pornography that reveals an image of women that is strikingly similar to what purity culture would like women to be.

Take Real Dolls, for example. These dolls—which their distributor publicizes as "the most realistic love doll in the world"—are life-size sex mannequins that look disconcertingly like, well, real women. The dolls have articulated skeletons (for "anatomically correct positioning," says the website[9]) and three orifices. Buyers can choose from ten body types, sixteen interchangeable faces, and different wigs, makeup, and even pubic hairstyles. For all of this customization and use of high-end materials, consumers pay about $6,500 per doll.* There is even a community of men online who call themselves iDollators—they discuss their real dolls, post pictures of them, and run a monthly web magazine, *Cover Doll*.[10]

In an article for Salon.com, reporter Meghan Laslocky spent months on iDollator forums and websites, talking to men (online and off) about their Real Dolls. One website, which she called "Hello Dolly" to protect the users of the forum, is nearly twelve thousand members strong—Laslocky called it "a place where all my worst fears about men churned in an awful froth."

> *Here were thousands of men who love the idea of peeling a woman's face off and replacing it with another, who revel in taking pornographic photographs of their "girlfriends" and sharing them with their friends, men who glory in sex unfettered by the daily push-pull of a relationship, men who might have little respect for the word "no."*[11]

---

* For the thrifty Real Doll purchaser, headless, limbless torsos run just $1,299.

And, in what seems like a natural next step for men who see plastic dolls as perfect women, Real Doll users often find ways to abuse their dolls. When Laslocky interviewed a Real Doll repairman, he spoke about badly mutilated dolls with their breasts hanging off, their hands and fingers severed. Another entrepreneurial type started a website to "rent out" Real Dolls. "Imagine love making for as long as you want and only in the ways that you want," reads the site. "A doll that looks a bit like Britney Spears poses and 'says,' 'I am Tracy and I will make your wishes come true. With me everything is at your pace. I never say 'no' and it is super easy to rent some time with me.'"[12]

In this way, these dolls are the pornographic expression of the ethics of passivity that real-life women are expected to adhere to. In fact, they're exactly what the purity myth would like women to be: passive, silent, and unable to articulate their desires.

As one Real Doll owner said to Laslocky, "For the most part, it's just like sex with an organic woman . . . who doesn't say anything and is brimful of Quaaludes." It's not surprising, then, that these iDollators don't refer to their dolls as sex toys* or masturbatory aides, but as "girlfriends." It's a sad state of affairs when some men would rather form intimate "relationships" with plastic dolls that can't reciprocate affection, engage in conversation, or do anything, really, than take the time to get to know actual women. (With pesky things like opinions and personalities, who wants to bother?)

While Real Doll buyers and iDollators may be on the fringe of sex toy aficionados—even twelve thousand members of a doll-fan website is not a tremendous number compared with the membership of other kinds of Internet pornography forums—there's no doubt that they have become part

---

* I'm not anti sex toy. I am anti treating plastic dolls as if they were real women and wishing real women were like plastic dolls.

of current American culture. The 2007 movie *Lars and the Real Girl* focused on the relationship between a disturbed man and his Real Doll; the dolls have been featured in articles and TV segments, and are a regular part of Howard Stern's radio-show shtick. There was even a *New York Daily News* gossip item about Charlie Sheen destroying and disposing of his Real Doll: "He and his bodyguard tried to dispose of it, like it was a real body. They wrapped it in a blanket and drove around in the middle of the night till they found a [D]umpster."[13]

There are other kinds of sex toys—thousands, in fact—so why the fascination with this particular doll? Perhaps the uncomfortable truth is that we're captivated by the Real Doll because it represents a trend in the United States: valuing women for their silence and inability to say no (or to say anything!) and seeing them as sex objects above all else.

Another part of the new world of porn that reveals volumes about the purity/porn connection is the cult of personal celebrity. A 2007 Pew Research Center poll reported that 51 percent of eighteen- to twenty-five-year-olds surveyed said that being famous is their generation's most important or second most important life goal; 81 percent said the same thing about being rich. In a culture where reality television reigns supreme and the promise of online celebrity has everyone lining up for even fifteen seconds of fame, it's not surprising that young people would hold being famous in such high regard, and think of it as an attainable goal. And with blogs, YouTube, MySpace, Facebook, and other social networking tools being so pervasive, most young Americans have some sort of public identity online. In this new tech world, we're *all* in the spotlight—it's just a matter of how many people are looking at us.

Unfortunately, for younger women, being famous often means

being a sex symbol—or a sex symbol in training—and the "famous for be-ing famous" trend has made it easier than ever to attain that status. Take Tila Tequila, who gained renown through the Internet by posting barely dressed pinup-girl pictures of herself and earning the "most popular person on MySpace" position. Appearances in men's and porn magazines followed, and now Tequila has a popular reality show on MTV, *A Shot at Love with Tila Tequila,* on which both male and female would-be suitors court her.

The truth is, it's hard to think of *any* female celebrity who isn't sexual-ized in some way.* Even female celebrities whose acclaim has nothing to do with sex find that they have to be seen as sex objects in order to remain famous. In her book *Female Chauvinist Pigs,* Ariel Levy points out that in the weeks before the 2004 summer Olympic Games, female athletes, such as high-jumper Amy Acuff and swimmers Amanda Beard and Haley Cope, were featured near to totally nude in publications like *For Him Magazine* and *Playboy.*

> *The collective effect of these pictures of hot (and, in most cases, wet) girls with thighs parted, tiny, porny patches of pubic hair, and coy, naughty-girl pouts made it almost impossible to keep sight of the women's awesome physical gifts. But that may have been the whole point: Bimbos enjoy a higher standing in our culture than Olympians right now.*[14]

If Levy is correct (and I'd like to hold out *some* hope that she's not), then she explains why so many young women aim to be "hot—if not as a life's calling, at least as a goal for day-to-day living." Author and my Feministing

---

* Even celebrities deemed too "old" or "ugly" are sexualized by public chatter about their general unhotness.

coblogger Courtney Martin wrote in her book *Perfect Girls, Starving Daughters* how this obsession is literally taking over many young women's lives:

> *The perfect girl focuses her energy on controlling her appearance. She spends her paycheck before the ink dries, buying trendy outfits that make her feel re-made. (Never mind that they will bore her before the month is out.) She compulsively buys makeup, gets a membership at the tanning salon, purchases the same pair of shoes in a variety of different colors—all so she can feel worthy of attention....* [15]

But the obsession with celebrity bimbos, as Levy calls them, and the struggle to be considered hot perpetuate the same fetishization of women that the virginity movement is built on. What's the difference between venerating women for being fuckable and putting them on a purity pedestal? In both cases, women's worth is contingent upon their ability to please men and to shape their sexual identities around what men want.

Celeb culture is akin to the spotlight shining on the virginity movement's purity princesses. Let's face it—the beauty queens and young girls touting virginity pledges are simply purity porn stars. Whether it's actual porn or mythologized purity, the end goal is to be desirable to men, and what women may actually want for themselves, sexually or otherwise, is lost.

PURITY'S PORN AGENDA

Concerned Women for America (CWA), a conservative Christian organization, wants to put an end to pornography—which CWA blames for everything from breaking up marriages to child-on-child rape.* But instead of

---

* All of the CWA's evidence is anecdotal.

talking about the content of porn or the health environment for sex workers, or even just plain old sexism, CWA zeroes in on Victoria's Secret and the former hit television show *Friends*. Really.

In a 2006 podcast, former chief counsel of CWA Jan LaRue bemoaned how CBS played lingerie label Victoria's Secret's runway show during a prime-time spot, and angrily mentioned how the *Friends* characters joke about looking at pornography. LaRue failed to mention any *actual* porn and instead focused on popular mainstream culture—like actresses posing partly nude on the cover of *Vanity Fair*. This is the virginity movement's version of antiporn activism.[16]

Even when fighting back against actual bad decisions, CWA can't help but throw in its two cents, which are always about sexual shaming. In a release about an Oklahoma court decision that freed a man after he was caught taking pictures up a sixteen-year-old girl's skirt (apparently, a teen in a mall has no "expectation of privacy"), the organization was sure to point out that the "teenager was not Britney Spears, Lindsay Lohan, or Paris Hilton out and about town sans panties."

"Unlike those celebrities, the teen was not dressed for and ready to be photographed getting out of cars without a care as to who sees what they are purposely revealing."[17] You know, girls who would be "asking for it."

That isn't to say CWA focuses on sexualization in pop culture only; it also targets corporations like hotel chains for providing pay-per-view porn, and seeks enforcement of state and federal obscenity laws. However, what it's striving for is not progressive change, but a return to "traditional" norms and a time when porn—widely defined as seemingly anything that's not women in head-to-toe prairie dresses and anything less chaste than hand holding—existed but was hidden from view and not discussed.* Ever.

---

* CWA seems concerned about any kind of progress—in its podcast on porn, LaRue also complained about iPods and portable DVD players.

And those obscenity laws CWA is fighting to uphold and enforce? Outside of being used to prosecute child pornographers—an honorable cause if there ever was one—these laws vary from state to state and more often than not center on pornography that strays from the heterosexual, "vanilla" norm. In 2005, for example, the FBI formed a "porn squad," an anti-obscenity crew of agents tasked with targeting pornography created for adults.*[18] They focused on (consensual) sadomasochistic porn, even arresting owners of an erotic-fiction website that featured just stories.[19]

Many anti-obscenity laws are so broadly interpreted that they have been used to ban the sale of sex toys in some states. In 2007, Alabama sex shop owners being targeted by anti-obscenity laws even tried to take their case to the Supreme Court, which refused to hear their challenge to the ban, so the law remained in place.[20] And in 2004, Joanne Webb, a Texas mother of three, was arrested for being a representative for passion parties—kind of like Tupperware parties, except the wares are vibrators rather than food containers.[21] Texas law actually does allow for the sale of sex toys, so long as they're described as novelty items. But when a person like Webb, also a former schoolteacher, explains what their actual role in sex is, she's *breaking the law.* Talk about a telling specification! Sex is fine so long as you're not talking about it seriously or openly.

This is the same reason the Independent Women's Forum (IWF), an antifeminist organization similar to CWA (but without the explicitly religious tilt), uses its campus program to try to stop on-campus productions of the award winning play *The Vagina Monologues*—which, the IWF says, "glorifies promiscuity and treats women as sex objects." It's not that the play says

---

* One FBI agent joked in *The Washington Post,* "I guess this means we've won the war on terror."[22]

anything particularly outrageous; the mere fact that "vagina" is in the title is enough to make it obscene.*[23] But it's really the fact that the play discusses—yes, in detail—female sexuality that gets the goat of virginity-movement organizations like IWF.

The Clare Boothe Luce Policy Institute, yet another organization that combats "obscenity," even published a booklet called "The Vagina Monologues Exposed: A Student's Guide to V-Day," which calls the play "humiliating" and "pornographic" and aims to help students protest their campus's productions. The "facts" the institute presents to discredit the play make little sense; for example, it describes one monologue that discusses masturbation as "exactly what the early suffragettes were fighting against."[24] And here I thought it was disenfranchisement! And when the organization gets into the nitty-gritty of why it believes the play is so pornographic, its underlying fear of female sexuality is clear.

> Myth #5: The play is not pornographic.
> False. It includes extremely graphic descriptions of women's sexual experiences. One monologue has an explicit depiction of two lesbians having sex. "She's inside me. I'm inside me" (Ensler 115). And it gets much more graphic. "The Vagina Workshop" describes one woman's experience with masturbation.[25]

The virginity movement's notions regarding obscenity and pornography have little to do with the actual issues in porn that affect women, such as hypermasculinity, humiliation, or violence against them. Gay sex or masturbation isn't what's harming women through porn—a hyped-up patriar-

---

* Because, as we all know, conservative women don't have vaginas.

chy is. After all, there's nothing "alternative" about calling women "whores" or presenting violence against women as sexual. That's good-old fashioned misogyny, and it's been around and systemically supported for a long time. That's why the purity pushers' objections to pornography are so hypocritical: They see it not as something that degrades women, but as something that degrades patriarchy and male control of female sexuality. If this isn't the case, then why the focus on masturbation and lesbian sex—two activities that are clearly very much under *women's* control?

The truth is that commercial pornography is exactly in line with the purity myth's values. In an article about the "raunch culture" that Levy discusses in her book, *In These Times* writer Lakshmi Chaudhry aptly notes that this porn culture "shift did not occur despite the rise of the religious Right but because of it."

> [M]ake no mistake, raunch is Republican. The sexuality that reigns supreme in Bush World bears the basic imprimaturs of right-wing ideology: gross materialism, sexual hypocrisy, and acquiescence in the name of empowerment. It is in every sense a conservative wet dream come true.[26]

And because this new porned America is actually a "conservative wet dream," the virginity movement is loath to change it, and would rather use it as an excuse to maintain the sexual status quo. Therefore, when groups like IWF or CWA call for an end to pornography, what they point to is never more realistic sexual images—it's chastity, the only acceptable answer.

The simple chaste "solution" has become so widespread that even some feminists are touting it. Naomi Wolf, for example, wrote a *New York* magazine piece on how men are becoming turned off by "real" women because of porn. Her suggestion seemed more like something Shalit would say than the woman who was arguably the '90s most famous feminist. She wrote about visiting an old friend, now an orthodox Jew in Jerusalem, who covered her head with a scarf.

> "Can't I even see your hair?" I asked, trying to find my old friend in there. "No," she demurred quietly. "Only my husband," she said with a calm sexual confidence, "ever gets to see my hair." ... And I thought: Our husbands see naked women all day—in Times Square if not on the Net. Her husband never even sees another woman's hair.[27]

The thing is, naked women aren't the problem—a woman believing her only value is sexual is what's dangerous. It's not women's sexuality that we have to watch out for, it's the way men construct it.

MOVING FORWARD IN A PORNED WORLD

This similarity between purity and porn culture—the way both fetishize women's sexual subservience—is what makes the virginity movement completely unable to analyze pornography in a progressive or helpful way. The movement has latched on to the mainstreaming of porn not because it cares about women and the way in which their sexuality is represented, but because porn is an easy scapegoat for what the movement perceives as society's ills (women having sex), as well as a convenient excuse to uphold the movement's regressive goals. The fact that conservative organizations conflate porn with sex toys, and masturbation and female pleasure with obscenity, reveals the true nature of their objections. These organizations blame progressive and feminist values because *that's* what they're fighting against—not real, tangible problems that affect women. So, instead of criticizing pornography from a perspective that seeks to help women, they end up reinforcing porn's sexist aspects. There's no doubt that the pornification of the United States affects young people adversely, but if young women are treating their bodies and sexuality as commodities, it's not because of porn culture—it's because of a larger societal message that tells them their sexuality is not their own.

But there's also no arguing that this new porn culture, raunch culture, or whatever one wants to call it merits analysis—be it political or moral. If they're doing it wrong, how do *we* do it right?

To start with, we must abandon the idea that women's bodies are inherently shameful, and that women's sexuality needs to be restricted. Some of the more recent measures to control pornography are mired in the state-as-pimp model. Through the Adam Walsh Child Safety and Protection Act, the U.S. Department of Justice generates a list of all actors in the porn industry. According to the 2007 rules, this list ensures that no minors are engaging in sex work, but infringing on a whole industry's freedom of privacy seems a bit extreme.

Instead of employing the naming-and-shaming technique, organizations and legislators should be using their collective power and funding to *talk to* those in the sex industry and not dismiss them out of hand. There are feminist and pro-woman porn makers and performers who are working to make the industry better for women every day. Connecting with them is a necessary first step.

We need to start, though, by *finding* those woman-friendly sex industry workers! In a culture where all things commercial and porned come with an appropriated feminist "empowered" label (think the Pussycat Dolls), it's difficult to parse what's woman-friendly and what's being marketed as such.

Take the popular company Suicide Girls—porn that features "alternative" women.* For a long time, the company enjoyed a high-profile reputation as female controlled and operated. John d'Addario, editor of the porn blog Fleshbot, noted that "the perception that women had an important/equal role in the administration of the site probably made it more attractive to some people who might not have visited a porn site otherwise." But in 2005, a group of ex–Suicide Girls starting bashing the company, saying that the female-empowerment front was a farce. About thirty models quit, claiming that Suicide Girls is actually controlled by a man, cofounder Sean Suhl, whom they accused of treating the workers poorly and underpaying them.

Mainstream porn establishments masquerading as feminist bastions aside, there is a long history of "pro-sex feminists,"† like Ellen Willis, Nina Hartley, Susie Bright, Annie Sprinkle, Betty Dodson, Audacia Ray, and Tristan Taormino, who do the hard work of talking about porn in a nuanced, multifaceted way.

And with the advent of the Internet, feminist women—many of whom make a distinction between mainstream pornography and *all* pornography—are talking progressively about porn more and more. Take blogger Andrea Rubenstein (a.k.a. tekanji), who wrote, "I am pro in its most basic form (material that arouses), but anti-mainstream . . . anti-industry, and anti-porn culture. . . . The difference between me and anti-porn feminists is that I believe that, while hard, it is not impossible to have pornography in this culture that doesn't objectify/degrade the participants."[28]

In her book, *Naked on the Internet: Hookups, Downloads, and Cashing In*

---

* In this case, "alternative" means lots of tattoos and body piercing, and some variety in body size and shape.

† Though I have to say, I don't know any "antisex" feminists!

on Internet Sexploration, Audacia Ray wrote that "women over the last decade or so have stared to remake, question, challenge, and enjoy the adult industry in a way that perhaps is only possible with the assistance of increasingly user-friendly and inexpensive technology."[29]

Ray points out that while mainstream porn is run and created primarily by men, women "with the entrepreneurial and nudie spirit" are increasingly creating their own sites—something that wouldn't be possible without online advancements.

This isn't to say that I believe the Internet will be the answer to misogyny in porn—it's clear that online porn is a tremendous part of the problem. But women talking about it, and taking control of the industry, is definitely a first step.

The second step, of course, is to start ignoring the virginity movement's badly intentioned and even more poorly executed actions surrounding porn. We need to take back the idea of "morality" and sexuality. Why? Because the virginity movement has a stronghold on it and is using it to actively hurt women. And not just by ignoring the real problems; the movement is creating new ones. If we continue to allow it to use pornography as a way to make extreme ideas about women, chastity, and sexuality mainstream, we're supporting a system that devalues women even more than some of the worst porn does.

classroom chastity

"Each time a sexually active person gives that most personal part of himself or herself away, that person can lose a sense of personal value and worth. It all comes down to self-respect."

from the abstinence-only teachers' guide
CHOOSING THE BEST PATH[1]

PAM STENZEL HAS A ROOMFUL of teenagers laughing up a storm. In her educational video *Sex Has a Price Tag,* Stenzel cracks jokes while being engaging, authoritative, and convincing. Amidst her quips about sex and annoying parents, she tells the students—packed into what looks like a school auditorium—that birth control could kill them and that abortion can lead to anorexia and suicide. She follows with another joke, and the teens laugh some more.

For schools that can't afford Stenzel's $5,000 speaking fee, this video is the perfect substitute—part of an abstinence arsenal of dozens of DVDs, books, and brochures available on ShopPamStenzel.com. Stenzel is just one of hundreds of abstinence educators who speak in schools, churches, community groups—even government agencies—nationwide.

Another one of these educators is Christian comedian Keith Deltano, who performs his abstinence routine at Virginia high schools. His shtick involves tying up a male volunteer from the audience and dangling a cinder block precariously over his genital area to demonstrate the ineffectiveness of condoms against HIV/AIDS.[2]* Alabama-based speaker Janice Turner, who founded Power of Purity classes, explained her classroom philosophy to a reporter recently by saying, "Girls give in to sex not because they want sex—it's like a hug. If they can get that from their fathers, they won't need it from a boyfriend."†

These are the virginity movement's front-liners, spreading the purity message in force.

Abstinence-only education—which includes sex education curricula, speakers like Stenzel and friends, peer educators, and various kinds of abstinence events#—is arguably the virginity movement's most successful venture to date. It's widespread, well funded, and becoming more and more mainstream—but not without consequences. The pervasiveness of abstinence-only programs ensures that a generation of young Americans has been indoctrinated not only with messages about how wrong, dirty, and immoral premarital sex is, but also with subjective—and often false—information: that contraception is ineffective (and sometimes dangerous), abortion is wrong, and any sexual activity outside of marriage is likely to make them diseased, poor, depressed, and suicidal.

---

* I'm betting the actual lesson learned is to steer clear of bad comics brandishing bricks.
† There are lots of things I imagine young girls would like to get from their dads—a phone call, advice about what to get their mom on her birthday, a pizza and ice-cream night—but I'm guessing a stand-in for sex isn't one of them.
# Like purity balls or a visit from the local crisis pregnancy center!

In Jeniann's ninth-grade sex ed class in Virginia Beach, Virginia, her teacher told her and her fellow students that it was against the law to have premarital sex.

"She told us if we did it and were caught, we could face fines, probation, and possibly jail time," Jeniann, now sixteen, emailed me.

"She said it had to be illegal because premarital sex undermines the family, which is a necessary thing in society."

Morgan Dickens, a twenty-two-year-old woman I met while visiting Cornell University in upstate New York, told me that at her San Antonio, Texas, high school, teachers weren't even allowed to *mention* words that related to anything but abstinence.

"Our biology teacher told us she couldn't say anything about birth control when a girl asked how it worked." Dickens also recalled that a student in her health class was actually kicked out of the room and asked to sit outside because he mentioned something about STIs and using a condom.

Many of the young people I've spoken to—whether via email, through Feministing.com, or on college campuses—have told me how abstinence programs use fear- and shame-based tactics to spread their misinformation. Katelyn Bradley of Florida, for example, wrote me an email detailing her middle school health class's exercise on abstinence: "They asked for several volunteers, and the woman leading the discussing held a wrapped gift. We weren't supposed to give away this gift until after marriage. If we had sex before marriage, our special present (sexuality) would be ruined. They literally demonstrated this notion in front of the class by passing it along the line of volunteers, with each person stomping on the wrapped gift." I suppose if this educator thinks having premarital sex is akin to being stomped on, I can't really hold her abstinence leanings against her.

Cassandra Tapia, a twenty-one-year-old from Dallas, emailed me about her seventh-grade abstinence-class teacher, who started one of her lessons by yelling, "Sex feels good!"

"She also made us say it," Tapia told me. "Then she told us a story about 'Ken' and 'Barbie,' using Velcro gloves as visuals. She talked about how Ken and Barbie dated and hung out, and then—with a dramatic slamming of the Velcroed hands together—had sex. Then she showed us how it was possible to separate her hands, but it was difficult and made a painful ripping noise."

Sadly, these young women's experiences aren't anomalous. It's not only oddball teachers who are lying to and intimidating students; these tactics are written into schools' curricula. A 2004 report from Representative Henry Waxman (D-CA) indicated that over 80 percent of federally funded abstinence programs contain false or misleading information about sex and reproductive health.[3]

The report found that all of the curricula studied failed to provide information on how to select a birth control method and use it properly; that it greatly exaggerated the failure rate of condoms in pregnancy prevention; and that it flat-out propagated inaccuracies by discounting (or even outright denying) condoms' effectiveness in preventing STD and HIV transmission. According to the report:

> One curriculum draws an analogy between the HIV virus and a penny and compares it to a sperm cell ("Speedy the Sperm"), which on the same scale would be almost 19 feet long. The curriculum asks, "If the condom has a failure rate of 14% in preventing 'Speedy' from getting through to create a new life, what happens if this guy (penny) gets through? You have a death: your own."[4]

Other curricula provided false information about pregnancy risks in sexual activity outside of intercourse—one text even states that merely touching another person's genitals can cause pregnancy. The bad science and misleading statistics go on and on: One program teaches that HIV can be transmitted through tears, while another falsely links abortion with sterility, mental retardation, and premature births in future pregnancies.[5]

Martha Kempner, vice president of information and communications at the Sexuality Information and Education Council of the United States (SIECUS), a New York–based organization that advocates for accurate and comprehensive education on sex and reproductive health, told me that this type of misinformation is just the tip of the abstinence iceberg. "They're attacking a way of living, and their brand of sex ed has very little to do with sex—it's a social message."

SIECUS has been keeping track of abstinence-only education programs and dissecting their curricula for years, and some of the teachings the organization has found aren't just wrong—they're terrifying. One commonly used book says, "Relying on condoms is like playing Russian roulette."[6] Another reads, "AIDS can be transmitted by skin-to-skin contact."[7]

These programs aren't just spreading medical and scientific misinformation, either—they're also sending social and values-based messages. A popular abstinence text, "Sex Respect," warns students of the dire consequences of premarital sex: "[I]f you eat spoiled food, you will get sick. If you jump from a tall building, you will be hurt or killed. If you spend more money than you make, your enslavement to debt affects you and those whom you love. If you have sex outside of marriage, there are consequences for you, your partner, and society."[8]

"This is a social agenda masquerading as teen pregnancy prevention,"

Kempner said. "They're going so far backwards on the messages they're giving women—that purity is the most important thing and what you should be striving for is a wedding. Saying that the most important thing you can do is get married and have children isn't the most empowering message."

Empowerment is indeed not the goal of abstinence-only curricula, which are built on outdated notions of gender norms and sexist stereotypes about sexuality and relationships, and ultimately seek a return to traditional gender norms. The virginity movement has a captive audience in middle school and high school classes, and it's planning on using that to its full advantage—why stop at condom-failure rates when you can fit a whole ideology in there?

The social messages of abstinence-only education are nothing if not old school. Women are often described as weak, intellectually inferior, and needing men's financial and physical protection.

In Waxman's report, one text was said to have listed "financial support" as one of the "5 Major Needs of Women," and "domestic support" as one of the "5 Major Needs of Men."[9] Another describes how girls don't "focus" as well as boys: "Generally, guys are able to focus better on one activity at a time and may not connect feelings with actions. Girls access both sides of the brain at once, so they often experience feelings and emotions as part of every situation."[10]

The pivotal moment for me—the moment when I realized how little abstinence proponents value women's intellect—was when I came across a pink glitter–decorated girls' T-shirt on an abstinence website, decorated with the message SEX CAUSES BABIES in a fun font.[11] Just in case you weren't aware.

Some teachings don't even bother to hide the degree to which *extremely* antiquated notions—like viewing women as property—are being pushed.

Why kNOw, an abstinence-only textbook, outlines this instruction to abstinence teachers: "Tell the class that the Bride price is actually an honor to the bride. It says she is valuable to the groom and he is willing to give something valuable for her."[12] The same book also notes, "The father gives the bride to the groom because he is the one man who has had the responsibility of protecting her throughout her life. He is now giving his daughter to the only other man who will take over this protective role."[13]

Another popular notion in abstinence curricula is that women don't like sex (and if they do, something must be amiss*). Because women aren't as prone to what these texts describe as "practical enslavement to one's sexual drive" as men are, it's the girls' job to keep the boys at bay.

A workbook from *Sex Respect* states, "Because they generally become aroused less easily, females are in a good position to help young men learn balance in relationships by keeping intimacy in perspective." Another notes, "Girls need to be aware they may be able to tell when a kiss is leading to something else. The girl may need to put the brakes on first in order to help the boy."[14] Because, according to the virginity movement, men have no self-control when it comes to anything sexual. Yet another abstinence book claims, "A woman is far more attracted by a man's personality, while a man is stimulated by sight. A man is usually less discriminating about those to whom he is physically attracted."[15] And no, these textbooks are *not* from the 1950s.

When women *are* accorded a sex drive, it's generally attributed to the increased sexualization of pop culture interfering with their natural disdain

---

* Texts often attribute girls' "promiscuity" (i.e., having any premarital sex) to low self-esteem, depression, or attention-seeking behavior. It's never described as a natural or pleasurable urge.

for intercourse: "[A] young man's natural desire for sex is already strong due to testosterone. . . . Females are becoming culturally conditioned to fantasize about sex as well."

Making women the sexual gatekeepers and telling men they just can't help themselves not only drives home the point that women's sexuality is unnatural, but also sets up a disturbing dynamic in which women are expected to be responsible for men's sexual behavior.

A passage in *Sex Respect* reads, "A guy who wants to respect girls is distracted by sexy clothes and remembers her for one thing. Is it fair that guys are turned on by their senses and women by their hearts?" Another classroom activity I learned about through SIECUS involved the story of Stephanie and Drew, a couple trying to save sex until marriage. Stephanie is too affectionate and wears tight clothing: "Drew likes her a lot, but lately keeping his hands off her has been a real job!" Stephanie has made it clear that she doesn't want to have sex; "her actions, however, are not matching her words."[16]

Sounds a bit like "no means yes," "look what she was wearing," and various other rape-apologist excuses. When abstinence curricula contain information about sexual abuse or assault (though they often don't), the message is similar: The onus of preventing sexual assault is on girls—not on men.

SIECUS's "No More Money for Abstinence-Only-Until-Marriage Programs" project notes that classes portray abstinence as a choice—which, considering the high rates of rape and sexual assault among young people,* it often just isn't.

---

* Eighty-five thousand cases of child sexual abuse are *reported* every year.[17]

Federal guidelines for abstinence-only-until-marriage programs associate sexual abstinence with all things virtuous and sexual activity with a life doomed to failure. Not only is this untrue, but it serves to inflict greater harm upon those who have survived coerced sexual behavior. Such messages are likely to cause further feelings of hurt, shame, anger, and embarrassment in these already victimized young people.[18]

In addition to shaming sexual-assault victims, positioning abstinence as women's domain further promotes the notion that it's women's morality that's on the line when it comes to sex—men just can't help themselves, so their ethics are safe from criticism.

Other young people suffering under these discriminatory teachings are LGBTQ youth, who are outright ignored or ostracized. Queer sexuality is not discussed at all; in fact, federal guidelines for abstinence-only programs make even mentioning gay sex near impossible.

In 2006, the United States Department of Health and Human Services' Administration for Children and Families (ACF) created new guidelines for organizations applying for grants to support abstinence-only education programs. These rules mandated that curricula were to define sexual abstinence very specifically, as "voluntarily choosing not to engage in sexual activity until marriage . . . sexual activity refers to any type of genital contact or sexual stimulation between two persons including, but not limited to, sexual intercourse."[19] Educators were also required to define the term "marriage" as only "a legal union between one man and one woman as a husband and wife," and the word "spouse" as only "a person of the opposite sex who is a husband or a wife." Since, according to the virginity movement, only married people are "allowed" to have sex, queer students are essentially taught that sexual intimacy is something they can never experience.*[20] For students who may have gay friends or family members, the message is similar: Their loved ones don't exist.

And, of course, for heterosexual teens who are already sexually active, the only information available to them is all false statistics meant to shame them.

Despite its history of fear-based messaging and regressive goals, abstinence education is becoming decidedly more upbeat as of late. Perhaps recognizing that herpes slideshows and threats of cinder blocks to the crotch weren't quite cutting it, abstinence educators are now pumping up the "youth" factor in their presentations.

Bringing in peer educators, hip-hop groups, and comedians has become par for the course in recent years. As has a healthy dose of consumerism— why let MTV have all the fun? Students can buy shirts proclaiming their virginal status with messages like CHASTEGIRL, CHASTE COUTURE, and (my personal favorite) NO TRESPASSING ON THIS PROPERTY, MY FATHER IS WATCHING.[21] Abstinence Clearinghouse also sells promise rings, posters, bookmarks—anything you can think to slap a purity message on is there for the buying.

Abstinence leaders are joining in on the fun, too. In a continued effort to revamp its scaremonger image into something more mainstream, the annual conference for abstinence educators, organized by the Abstinence Clearinghouse, decided to have annual themes. In 2006, it was a *Wizard of Oz* conference, complete with panel titles like "If I Only Had a Brain: The Effects of Sex on Brain Physiology," "A Horse of a Different Color,"† and "Ding, Dong, the

---

* Unless they want to remain closeted and marry someone of the opposite sex, of course— a popular course of action for some Republican lawmakers these days.

† This panel title is for a group of hip-hop dancers. Ahem.

Witch Is Dead! Which Old Witch? (The 'Safe-Sex' Witch)."[22] To further avoid being perceived as out of touch with youth culture (because what says "hip" like a movie from 1939?), the 2008 conference hosted a contest called Abstinence Idol: "Performances can include the following, but are not limited to: singing, drama, oratory, pantomime."*[23] And who among us can deny the draw of chastity-based pantomime?

But whether it's by using comedians or Velcro gloves, retro textbooks or ruby slippers, these programs are working hard, and not just to get teens to hold off on sex until marriage. Abstinence-only education seeks to create a world where everyone is straight, women are relegated to the home, the only appropriate family is a nuclear one, reproductive choices are negated, and the only sex people have is for procreation.

CHASTITY CASH

Though controversy over abstinence-only education, as well as criticism thereof, are fairly recent—the Bush administration's sex-education policies made it quite a popular subject—this kind of "teaching" has been alive, kicking, and well endowed for over twenty years.

Abstinence-only education programs have received more than $1.3 billion dollars since 1996; they're currently slated to receive $176 million in federal funding in 2008.[24] But abstinence education was really born in 1981, thanks to the passage of the Adolescent Family Life (AFL) Act under the Reagan administration.† The AFL authorized the funding of pregnancy

---

* For this reason alone, I tried my darnedest to gain admission to the 2008 conference. Alas, security was tight, and they weren't letting in any known anti–abstinence education writers.

† It was widely referred to as the Chastity Act, just in case there was any question about its purpose.

prevention programs, but only those that offered abstinence as the only appropriate course of action—no money was to be given to programs that "encouraged" abortion.[25]

Because the AFL's programs often advocated specific religious values, the American Civil Liberties Union filed suit in 1983, claiming that the programs violated the separation of church and state. After a decade-long court battle, a 1993 settlement forbade AFL-funded programs to include religious references and required the information they dispensed to be medically accurate, among other stipulations.

The virginity movement's next win happened in 1996, when a provision attached to the welfare-reform act allotted $50 million a year for five years for abstinence-only programs. (The states that choose to accept those funds are required to match every four federal dollars with three state dollars.)[26]

The programs that use these funds must follow an eight-point definition (often called the A-H guidelines) of what appropriate abstinence education is. The requirements include program participants' teaching students that "sexual activity outside of marriage is likely to have harmful psychological and physical effects," and that "bearing children out-of-wedlock is likely to have harmful consequences for the child, the child's parents, and society."[27]

In addition to its endorsement by the AFL and its funds earmarked through welfare reform,[28] abstinence-only education receives funding from the Community-Based Abstinence Education Program (CBAE), created in 2001 by conservatives in the House of Representatives. CBAE is controlled by the Administration for Children, Youth, and Families and is the strictest—and perhaps most damaging—form of abstinence funding: Under it, grants often go to private, faith-based organizations like crisis pregnancy centers. Grantees *must* teach all eight points of the abstinence A-H guidelines, *must* target children ages twelve to eighteen, and absolutely cannot provide students with any positive information about contraception. Naturally, the virginity movement is a big fan of CBAE subsidies; since the program's inception in 2001, funding has increased by 465 percent and reached a whopping $113 million in 2007.[29]

THE PLAYERS

So who are these elusive leaders of the virginity movement? The major players are the Abstinence Clearinghouse and the National Abstinence Education Association (NAEA). They're the leading lobbyists, organizations, and providers of "educational" material in the United States. And while proponents of abstinence education run the gamut from legislators to community leaders, it's large organizations like these, and their powerful ties to conservative Christian think tanks (and more), that make them so very influential.

The National Advisory Council for the Abstinence Clearinghouse, for example, includes members from Focus on the Family, the Heritage Foundation, and numerous crisis pregnancy centers. The organization, which receives more than half a million dollars a year in government grants and contracts, also has a strictly anti-choice medical abstinence board, which must "not only support abstinence-only-until-marriage programs" but also not "counsel, prescribe, or distribute condoms or contraceptives to youth."[30] (In addition to its connection to the abstinence movement, the organization has ties to campaigns that aim to limit access to the HPV vaccine and contraception.)

Perhaps the most important aspect about the Clearinghouse is that Leslee Unruh, arguably the most well-known leader of the abstinence and anti-choice movements, heads it. Unruh, who gained national attention in 2006 when she was campaigning in South Dakota for a ban on abortion (even in cases of rape and incest), frequently makes the rounds on radio and cable television, touting abstinence-only education and deriding abortion, birth control, and premarital sex. Her debating style is quite . . . original. A 2007 Fox News segment featured Unruh and Mary Alice Carr, of NARAL Pro-Choice New York, debating over a new oral contraceptive called Lybrel. After arguing that the birth control pill was poison and that women needed to be protected from it, Unruh ended the segment by shouting over Carr, "I want more babies. More babies! We love babies!"[31]

Unruh loves babies so much, in fact, that she founded an organization called the Alpha Center, which aims to convince women not to have abortions. In 1987, the Alpha Center pled no contest to five misdemeanor charges of unlicensed adoption and foster care practices. (Nineteen charges, including four felonies, were dropped.) Tim Wilka, the state's attorney in Minnehaha County, South Dakota, at the time, told the *Argus Leader,* "There were so many allegations about improper adoptions being made [against Unruh] and how teenage girls were being pressured to give up their children. . . . Gov. George Mickelson called me and asked me to take the case."[32] Apparently, Unruh had been promising pregnant teens money to stay pregnant so she could later put their children up for adoption.

The NAEA doesn't have a much better record. In 2007, the organization, whose board comprises a virtual who's who of abstinence education, hired the public relations firm Creative Response Concepts—known for the 2004 Swift Boat Veterans ads slamming John Kerry—to spearhead a PR campaign for abstinence-only education policies. In 2006, NAEA executive director Valerie Huber, the head of Ohio's abstinence programs, was suspended after a state ethics investigation found her guilty of neglect of duty for hiring a company she was affiliated with to do state work.[33]

Another abstinence organization, Heritage Community Services (which runs after-school abstinence programs and training workshops for teachers and sells abstinence-only curricula), receives a staggering $3 million a year in government contributions and grants. Like the Clearinghouse and the NAEA, Heritage's leadership is wrought with ethical red flags. The women's legal-rights organization Legal Momentum* reports that the Heritage curriculum is produced and sold by Badgley Enterprises, a for-profit company run by Heritage founder and CEO Anne Badgley and her husband.

> Heritage Community Services purchases its Heritage Keepers textbooks from Badgley Enterprises. Public records show that Badgley Enterprises earned $174,201 from the sale of its textbooks to Heritage in 2004, and that Badgley herself earned $51,000 as a writer for Badgley Enterprises. Additionally, Badgley's husband, daughter, and son-in-law are all paid Heritage employees. Accusations have also been made that Badgley Enterprises was used as a personal account for various members of the Badgley family.[34]

In addition, it came out that the organization had paid $11,000 in 2002 to send two South Carolina state employees to an abstinence conference in California. Badgley defended the decision by calling the trip "inexpensive."[35]

These organizations and leaders have strong ties to the anti-choice movement and conservative Christian groups. They have no place in public schools, yet the power they wield over American youth, even in our public schools, is a little more than unnerving.

---

* Where I had my first job out of grad school (in the interest of full disclosure).

This abstinence-only world is a far cry from reality (residing somewhere in Oz, perhaps?), and not even close to what people want for themselves and their children. According to a study published in *Pediatrics & Adolescent Medicine,* 82 percent of Americans support programs that teach contraception as well as abstinence, and half of all Americans oppose abstinence-only education altogether. Even among those who describe themselves as conservatives, 70.percent support comprehensive sex education.[36]

Some parents—those who aren't about to sit back and watch their kids get taught that condoms don't work and sex is dirty—*are* fighting back. The wonderful documentary *Abstinence Comes to Albuquerque* follows the story of a New Mexico mom, Susan Rodriguez, who was outraged when she found out that a faith-based private organization—funded by federal dollars—was teaching her daughter about sex.*[37] Rodriguez went to the Albuquerque school board in 2005 and started complaining, and more and more people in the community took notice. Community members, local politicians, and lawmakers made enough of a fuss that, after a yearlong fight, the state stopped funding these programs in middle and high schools.

One mother, Kristin Phillips, told me in an email that her daughter came home complaining about an STD assembly she was required to attend when she was a sophomore at a Missouri high school.

"The woman leading the assembly told them calculated untruths and

---

* Another thing that really struck me while watching this film was how an organization composed of mostly white, Christian women was deciding what young women of color—many of them poor—would learn about appropriate sexual behavior and what constitutes a family. Many children in New Mexico come from single-parent homes (bad!); some of them may have parents who aren't straight (sin!).

misleading statements about how condoms have very high failure rates, and [said] there was no reason to get the HPV vaccine," Phillips wrote.

Phillips discovered the program violated state law, which required sex ed teachers to provide medically accurate information and contraceptive options, and that parents be notified about and informed of the content of any sex ed programs their children would be attending.

"I was directed to the school nurse who was in charge of setting up this program every year," Phillips continued. "I told her I was concerned about the things the students had been told, and that I had a problem with [their] being given false information about contraception and the HPV vaccine. I pointed out that the district was in violation of the state law, but she said that was 'my interpretation.'"

Rodriguez and Phillips are not the only parents fighting back—thank goodness. The Internet—teens' public forum of choice—makes calling out misinformation easier, especially for young people. One student, wary of an abstinence lecture at his high school in Spencer, Iowa, filmed the presentation with his cell phone and posted it on YouTube. In addition to telling run-of-the-mill lies about contraception and STIs to the adolescent audience, the lecturer claimed, "The base of most of the lipstick sold in our stores comes from aborted babies."*[38] The video made the rounds on political blogs, exposing abstinence programs' outrageousness even further.

On Facebook, users have created over 150 groups dedicated to shining a light on how dangerous and illogical abstinence-only education is, including popular groups like Abolish Abstinence-Only Education—which has nearly one hundred thousand members and posts action items, news alerts, and

---

* Apparently, the virginity movement is not just concerned with the high rates of teen sex—it's combating the evils of Bonne Bell Lip Smackers as well!

informational-website links—and the more irreverent "Abstinence only sex education is just like hold it potty training."

Political and feminist blogs have taken abstinence-only education to task time and time again, whether it's RH Reality Check calling out corrupt abstinence leadership or Feministing.com covering the legislative angles while mocking the bad T-shirts.[39]

Abstinence-only programs have also been criticized by organizations ranging from the Society of Adolescent Medicine—which called the abstinence curricula "ethically problematic" and a threat to "fundamental human rights to health, information, and life"—to the American Psychological Association.[40] But despite all of the political, organizational, and community outrage over abstinence-only education, the programs continue to be funded—heavily.

THE END OF ABSTINENCE?

Thankfully, there does seem to be a light at the end of the abstinence-only tunnel. In addition to concerned parents, teens, and progressive organizations, state governments and school boards are catching on. To date, almost half of the fifty states have refused federal abstinence dollars, namely because of the way those subsidies limit schools' ability to talk about contraception—and all the evidence indicates that more states will join them.[41]

But that doesn't mean abstinence proponents are going anywhere—far from it. In early 2008, the NAEA launched a $1 million campaign called Parents for Truth, the goal of which is to enlist one million parents to support abstinence-only education by lobbying school boards and lawmakers.[42] The organization timed the campaign to coincide with Congress's debate over whether to authorize approximately $190 million in federal abstinence funds.

Not surprisingly, there's not much truth telling going on in this campaign—its website's headlining video reports that comprehensive sex education tells children it's okay to take showers with each other and instructs them on how to give partners orgasms.

James Wagoner, president of Advocates for Youth, an organization that helps young people make informed and responsible decisions about their reproductive and sexual health, calls this characterization of comprehensive sex education "absolutely misleading." In an interview *The Washington Post*, Wagoner noted that Parents for Truth is "a classic fear and smear campaign."[43] Par for the course for abstinence proponents, of course, and for the virginity movement as a whole.

No matter how successful abstinence leaders might be, and whether they continue to receive funding or not, Americans are nonetheless going to have to deal with cleaning up the mess that abstinence-only education leaves in its wake. After all, we can't teach false statistics and medically inaccurate information for twenty years and expect that a generation of young people will be just fine.

A 2007 study Congress ordered found that middle school students who had received abstinence-only education were just as likely to have sex as teenagers as those who had not. The same report showed that the teens who had taken abstinence classes were more likely to say that condoms were ineffective in protecting people against STIs—over 20 percent said that condoms can never protect against HIV.[44] So if students who take abstinence classes are just as likely to have sex as their peers, but have less information about how to protect themselves from pregnancy and STIs—or, worse, believe they cannot prevent pregnancy and STIs at all—that leaves them completely unprotected.

It makes sense, then, that a 2005 report showed that teenagers who took abstinence-only education classes and pledged their virginity were not only less likely to use condoms, but also more likely to engage in oral and anal sex.[45]

Clearly, this isn't what we want for young people. What these students are proving is that the shaming and scaring isn't working. Less information isn't helping—it's hurting.

I'm not going to reinforce the "they're going to do it anyway"* argument. I believe it's time to take a stance on sex education that isn't so passive—young people deserve accurate and comprehensive sex education not just because they're going to have sex, but because *there's nothing wrong with having sex.* Allowing educators to equate sexuality with shame and disease is not the way to go; we are doing our children a great disservice. Not only are we lying to them, we're also robbing them of the joy that a healthy sex life (as a teenager or in adulthood) can provide.

Young people deserve to be equipped to make well-informed decisions for themselves. Enough with teaching young women that they're somehow "ruined" if they become sexually active. Enough with telling students that sexuality is shameful. Enough. I'm reminded of the title of the Abstinence Clearinghouse's 2007 annual conference: "Abstinence Is a Black & White Issue: Purity vs. Promiscuity." That's what we're fighting against—it's time we inserted some nuance and empathy into this national disaster we call sex education.

---

* Which, of course, they will.

legislating sexuality

"A real-life description to me would be a rape victim, brutally raped, savaged. The girl was a virgin. She was religious. She planned on saving her virginity until she was married. She was brutalized and raped, sodomized as bad as you can possibly make it, and is impregnated."

BILL NAPOLI,
Former South Dakota Senator, responding to a question about what kind of woman should be "allowed" to have an abortion

IN LATE 2006, Ohio-based blogger Biting Beaver wrote about being denied emergency contraception. Her partner's condom had broken late that Friday night, so she called doctors, hospitals, and local clinics looking for the pill that could stop her from getting pregnant. Everyone turned her down.

I was told by every urgent care I called and every emergency room that I was shit out of luck. I was asked my age. My marital status. How many children I had. If I had been raped and when I became uncomfortable with the questions I was told, "Well Ma'am, try to understand that you will be interviewed and the doctor has 'criteria' that you need to meet before he will prescribe it for you."[1]

Already a mother of three children, Biting Beaver did not want to get pregnant again. But because she hadn't been raped (and wouldn't say that she had), she couldn't find a provider to give her this over-the-counter, *legal* contraceptive. It took her until early the following week to find someone who would give her the morning-after pill, and as it turned out, it was too late. Biting Beaver later informed her readers that she had indeed gotten pregnant and would now be scheduling an appointment to obtain an abortion.*

Her experience struck a chord, and soon news outlets were picking up the story. Other women writers and bloggers across the country started to share their stories of being denied contraception. Biting Beaver's experience, it seemed, was not uncommon.

Because of "refusal clause" laws (also called "conscience clause" laws)—which exist in some form in forty-seven states—healthcare providers, including doctors, pharmacists, and nurses, can deny women access to medication, procedures, or even referrals if the providers object morally to what's being asked of them.[2]† The laws are a tremendous win for the virginity movement, which believes that any form of contraception is wrong. After all, why should women be able to obtain prescriptions that make it easier for them to have premarital sex—something the movement believes women shouldn't be doing in the first place?

But this push to legislate chastity is much broader than just denying women birth control—there are laws that provide only married women with access to reproductive technology (such as in vitro fertilization), laws

---

* It's worth noting that coming forward with her story led to BB's being terribly harassed—she was derided and threatened in hundreds of comments and emails.
† Shockingly, it's not condoms, Viagra, or jock-itch medication that healthcare providers seem to have a problem with.

mandating that women take "marriage promotion" classes in order to receive their welfare benefits, and even laws that ban the sale of vibrators. While these issues may seem unrelated, they're all part of a larger agenda to control women's reproductive and sexual lives—reinforcing the idea that women must be chaste, even if that requires government intervention.

Recent rollbacks of women's political rights—especially reproductive rights—stem directly from the belief that women *shouldn't* have control over their own bodies. More and more, policy that affects women's bodies and rights is being formulated with the myth of sexual purity in mind. That's why rape victims are routinely treated more compassionately in abortion-rights conversations than women who have sex consensually are, and why legislation doesn't target women who fit into the perfect-virgin mold to the same degree as it does women who don't fulfill the stereotype—like low-income women and women of color. This is where the purity myth gets truly dangerous, because it's encroaching on our lives not just through social influences, but directly through legislation—legislation that's mired in fear of young women's sexuality, in paternalism, and in a need to punish women who aren't "pure."

OUR BODIES, THEIR LAWS

Over the last decade—thanks in no small part to the Bush administration—women's reproductive rights have decreased significantly. Not only has their right to obtain an abortion been endangered on both the state and the federal level, but there have also been continued assaults on birth control, and even on women's right to have children.

Cristina Page, author of *How the Pro-Choice Movement Saved America: Freedom, Politics, and the War on Sex,* told me, "You don't have to search too deeply on anti-abortion websites to find that the broad agenda entails stopping people from having sex outside of marriage or even within marriage if not for the purpose of procreation."

> The Pro-Life Activist's Encyclopedia *explains that just the notion of planning a pregnancy is heresy. It is their belief that attempting to plan a pregnancy is basically admitting you don't believe that God will provide. If you don't believe God will provide, well then you just don't believe. As Randall Terry, founder of Operation Rescue, explained, "If you are using birth control, stop. Let the number of children you have be decided by God." The goal of the pro-life movement is to strip us of the ability to prevent pregnancy and let the chips fall where they may.* [3]

While many Americans believe that women's reproductive health and rights are safe because of *Roe v. Wade,* the 1973 Supreme Court decision that legalized abortion, nothing could be further from the truth.

Between 1995 and 2007, states enacted 557 anti-choice measures—forty-three in 2007 alone. During George W. Bush's presidency, state legislatures considered more than 3,700 anti-choice measures in total.[4] These include parental notification and consent laws (legislation mandating that teenage girls get permission from their parents before they're permitted to obtain an abortion*), waiting periods, and even outright bans on the procedure. If *Roe* were overturned—not unlikely, given the Supreme Court justices' current leanings—thirty states would be ready to make abortion illegal within a year from that decision.[5]

In addition to the active danger of *Roe's* being repealed, American

---

* Not exactly an easy hurdle for girls with abusive parents or, as is, sadly, sometimes the case, girls whose father is responsible for the pregnancy.

women have a whole host of other legislative problems on their plate. A study by the Guttmacher Institute showed that as of 2008, 87 percent of U.S. counties had no abortion provider.[6] There are even some states, like Mississippi, that have only one abortion provider to serve the entire state.[7] This means that many women, especially those in rural areas, have to travel long distances to get to the nearest provider. Add mandatory waiting periods and misleading counseling about how abortion can cause breast cancer (and other false information), and all of a sudden, procuring an abortion doesn't seem like such an easily accessed right.

A woman in South Dakota who wants to get an abortion, for example, is subject to so many hurdles—geographic, financial, and legal—that getting an abortion is near impossible. Sarah Stoesz, president of Planned Parenthood Minnesota, North Dakota, South Dakota, says that in her region, the obstacles make some women so desperate that they take matters into their own hands.

Stoesz tells me the story of an eighteen-year-old living in western South Dakota who had an unplanned pregnancy. Because of financial constraints that prevented her from traveling across the state to the Planned Parenthood clinic in eastern South Dakota, this young woman inserted a toothpick into her cervix in desperation, hoping it would induce an abortion. After several days, she became afraid and called a local doctor to help her. The doctor informed her that removing the toothpick from her cervix might cause an abortion, so he refused to see her.

"There are many, many stories," says Stoesz. "Every week we hear another one."

Given all these stories, even calling abortion a "right" seems overly optimistic. After all, a right that can't be exercised is not very useful to anyone.

As Page points out, the anti-choice movement (whose agenda is so similar to the virginity movement's that the two seem inextricably linked) is hellbent not only on stopping women from using any form of contraception, but also on stopping them from having sex before marriage. Abortion is just one small part of a much larger goal.

For example, the virginity/anti-choice movements have recently moved beyond simply advocating for stricter abortion laws and limiting access to birth control—that would be too narrow-minded! Now they also want to tell pregnant women *how* to have their children.

In 2006, a Virginia lawmaker sponsored a bill to forbid unmarried women from using reproductive technology, such as in vitro fertilization, to get pregnant. The bill would have denied women without husbands access to "certain intervening medical technology" that "completely or partially replaces sexual intercourse as the means of conception."*

For women who already have children, the legislation is downright dangerous. In 2004, a Utah woman was charged with murder when one of her twin babies was stillborn after she refused to have a cesarean section. In South Carolina, Regina McKnight was convicted of homicide and sentenced to twelve years in prison after delivering a stillborn baby, because jurors believed the court's claim that her cocaine use had killed the child.† In 2006, lawmakers in Arkansas were considering making it a crime for pregnant women to smoke.[8]

This new crop of "fetal protection" laws has created a slippery slope for

---

* This is what I like to call the "no dick, no deal" law.
† After an eight-year-long court battle, the South Carolina Supreme Court overturned McKnight's conviction after finding that medical research linking cocaine to stillbirths is based on "outdated" medical information.

pregnant women, who are being thrown in prison simply for failing to give birth to a healthy baby.

Lynn Paltrow, executive director of the National Advocates for Pregnant Women, was quoted in a piece by Rick Montgomery as having said that this type of punishment is part of a larger trend. "I think thirty years of anti-abortion rhetoric—'women killing their babies'—has led to a moral vilification that doesn't just stick to those who seek to terminate a pregnancy. It's spreading to all pregnant women."[9]

Now, clearly, no one is arguing that pregnant women should be doing drugs, drinking, or smoking—but there's no question that these types of laws set a dangerous precedent. How long will it be before women are faulted for delivering stillborn babies because they didn't take prenatal vitamins, or because they drank the occasional glass of wine?

In 2006, the Centers for Disease Control and Prevention (CDC) released federal guidelines asking all women capable of conceiving to treat themselves as "pre-pregnant," even if they had no immediate plans to *get* pregnant. So if the above-mentioned hypothetical questions seem like a stretch, think again. If the CDC had its way, all women of reproductive age would "take folic acid supplements, refrain from smoking, maintain a healthy weight, and keep chronic conditions such as asthma and diabetes under control."[10]*

I'm all for staying healthy, but that's because I believe in taking care of myself—not in treating my body as a potential incubator at all times.

If you take some time to sift through the rhetoric of caring for women, "life," and concern for young women's sexual health, what you'll find in this

---

* The vessel will make sure to treat its uterus and surrounding matter with care for the preparation of the almighty fetus!

type of legislation is actually quite simple: an underlying fear of women's sexuality, an overwhelming need to control it, and an undercurrent of paternalism suggesting that women need protection from themselves—even if that means enforcing punitive measures to drive the point home.

YOU HAVE NOTHING TO FEAR BUT SEX ITSELF

While many—if not most—laws and policies concerning women's bodies reveal a fear of female sexuality, several stand out in the crowd.

Few examples demonstrate policymakers' far-reaching panic over young women's sexuality better than the three-year-long process the FDA underwent to approve emergency contraception (EC) for over-the-counter status (available without a prescription from a pharmacist) and the debates that surrounded it. The whole undertaking had all the intrigue of a mystery novel (or perhaps a bad made-for-TV movie): political deceit, resignations, arrests, and, most important, lots and lots of talk about teenage girls having sex.

The FDA approved EC—better known as the morning-after pill or by its brand name, Plan B—prescription use in 1998. The drug, which keeps women from getting pregnant by preventing or delaying ovulation,* started being pushed for over-the-counter availability by major medical associations in 2000, but the FDA didn't consider making the switch until June 2003.[11]

The FDA spent the next three years doing a bureaucratic dance in which it repeatedly delayed its decision and ignored expert after expert who

---

* The virginity movement argues that EC interferes with the implantation of a fertilized egg, and therefore ends a life. I can't muster up much empathy for a bunch of cells, or people who would trump cells' "rights" over an actual born person's, so I'm going with the medical and scientific definition of the drug.

supported EC's over-the-counter status. The biggest giveaway that politics trumped science happened in late 2003, when the FDA recommended that EC *not* be available for sale without a prescription, despite a recommendation from an independent joint advisory committee to the FDA to do so. (The committee recommended over-the-counter status in a 23–4 vote; the vote was 27–1 that the drug could be used safely by women of any age.[12]) The concerns that members of the FDA raised were mired in worries about women's sexuality—namely, that young women would become out of control if given the chance to have sex "without consequences."

Dr. W. David Hager, one of the FDA committee members who voted against EC's over-the-counter approval, told *The New York Times*: "What we heard today was frequently about individuals who did not want to take responsibility for their actions and wanted a medication to relieve those consequences."[13] This same man, an ob-gyn and published author who made waves when he suggested prayer as a cure for PMS, was one of the key players in making sure that the FDA rejected the committee's recommendation.[14]*

It later came to light that FDA medical official Janet Woodcock wrote in an internal memo that over-the-counter status could cause "extreme promiscuous behaviors such as the medication taking on an 'urban legend' status that would lead adolescents to form sex-based cults centered around the use of Plan B." That's right—sex-based cults.†

This line of reasoning may sound familiar. That's because it's the exact "concern" that was cited when the HPV vaccine was up for FDA approval,

---

* In addition to pushing Jesus as a cure-all for cramps, in 2005 Hager's former wife of thirty-two years accused him of regularly anally raping her. Just the kind of guy you want in charge of women's sexual lives!

† I told you this reeked of made-for-TV movie.

and the same excuse that legislators use to attempt to limit women's access to birth control.

For example, when a bill prohibiting University of Wisconsin campuses to provide students with any form of contraception passed in 2005, state representative Dan LeMahieu, who had introduced the legislation, told *The Capital Times* that he was "outraged that our public institutions are giving young college women the tools for having promiscuous sexual relations, whether on campus or thousands of miles away on spring break."*[15] I find it telling that Rep. LeMahieu sees access to contraception only as a means to a slutty end, rather than as young women's taking responsibility for their sexual health.

Ultimately, the FDA/EC debacle became a real crisis. In 2005, Susan Wood, director of the Office of Women's Health and assistant commissioner for women's health, resigned in protest. In an email sent to friends and colleagues, she wrote:

> *I have spent the last fifteen years working to ensure that science informs good health policy decisions....*
>
> *I can no longer serve as staff when scientific and clinical evidence, fully evaluated and recommended for approval by the professional staff here, has been overruled. I therefore have submitted my resignation effective today.*

Not until July 2006—after protests were launched and complaints lodged from female legislators and local activists (nine of whom got arrested in front of FDA headquarters), and the Government Accountability Office is-

---

* I love the idea that there *wouldn't* be wanton spring-break sex if campus health centers just stopped providing birth control. "No pills? Well, forget Daytona, gals—I'm headed straight to the library!"

sued a report about how politicized and "unusual" the process was—did the FDA approve EC for over-the-counter sale.[16]

Unfortunately, the drug was made available only to women aged eighteen and older, so the very people who need EC most—young women—were deprived. Once again, this restriction was conceived because of the FDA's fear that young women would misuse the drug and become "promiscuous."* Outside of being discriminatory, the age limit also made little sense. In many states, teen girls can obtain abortions without parental permission, but can't access a drug that can *stop them* from getting pregnant. So in New York, for example, if a teen girl has a broken-condom incident with her partner, she can't prevent a pregnancy using emergency contraception, but she *can* get an abortion should she become pregnant.

The FDA's approval process in this case is hardly the first (or the last, I imagine) time that the government's interference in women's health decisions has revealed the degree to which it's so fully entangled in fears about young females' sexuality. Deriding young women for having sex is a tradition with a long history, but when socially restrictive double standards about sex make their way into policy, we have an issue that isn't just women's problem—it's the country's problem.

DADDY KNOWS BEST

Another disturbing legislative theme hurting women—again, young women especially—is the widespread notion that women can't be trusted to make their own decisions.

---

* The FDA had no problem approving orlistat—a fat-blocking pill whose side effects include "fecal incontinence, gas, and oily discharge"—for all ages, despite the approval panel's concerns that younger people would misuse the drug. Apparently, a diet pill that makes you shit your pants is preferable to a safe form of contraception.

One of the most infuriating policy examples as far as this kind of paternalism is concerned is "informed consent" laws (also called Woman's Right to Know* laws), which, to date, thirty-three states implement to varying degrees. The premise of these laws is essentially that when a woman goes to get an abortion, she doesn't really know that she'll be . . . well, getting an abortion. Best that someone let her know—and in the most shaming way possible![17]

Informed consent laws, as they're supposed to, exist to ensure that people get accurate and unbiased information before receiving medical care so that they can make the decision that's best for them. But when it comes to abortion, the principles of informed consent go out the window. Laws that "inform" women about abortion often contain false, misleading, and/or biased information that seeks to shame and scare, rather than inform.

In South Dakota,† for example, the informed consent law requires doctors to tell women seeking abortions that the procedure "ends a human life," and "that the pregnant woman has an existing relationship with that unborn human being and that the relationship enjoys protection under the United States Constitution and under the laws of South Dakota."[18]

Sarah Blustain, who wrote about these laws for *The American Prospect*, notes just how condescending the legislation is:

> *This line of thinking makes clear that women are too ignorant to realize that they are carrying some sort of nascent life in them, and too weak to possibly decide for themselves whether to have an abortion. Even worse, draft-*

---

* You have to give the virginity movement credit: It certainly knows how to adopt prowoman rhetoric for antiwoman laws.

† Unfortunately for the women of SD, their state is the first place you should look when you want a good example of antiwoman legislation.

ers of the South Dakota law do not think women are competent to state whether they have absorbed all of this helpful state information properly: The law would require the doctor to certify, in writing, that he "believes she [the pregnant woman] understands the information imparted."[19]

A similar component of informed consent laws is ultrasounds—more specifically, requiring women to view an ultrasound before obtaining an abortion. (Again, so that they understand the whole "abortion" thing.)

Twelve states have an ultrasound-related requirement built into their abortion laws.[20] This means that the doctor is required to perform an ultrasound, and in some cases must ask the patient to view it. Disregard for the moment that an ultrasound requirement can add up to $200 to the already high cost of getting an abortion; what's even more distressing is that this requirement assumes, yet again, that women don't understand what an abortion is. And the reasoning behind the ultrasound requirement is definitely not coming from a place of informed consent. Its purpose is to shame women into thinking that if they *really* knew they were getting an abortion—"killing" a "separate" being—they wouldn't have one.

When Kansas senator Sam Brownback introduced the Ultrasound Informed Consent Act in 2007, which required women seeking abortions to have an ultrasound, he didn't say he was concerned that women weren't getting all the information they needed to make the best decision for themselves and their families. No, instead Senator Brownback said that he was hopeful that the bill would "cause a deeper reflection on the humanity of unborn children." *Deeper reflection*—because clearly, a woman who has taken a pregnancy test, found out she is unexpectedly pregnant, discussed her options with her family, decided to terminate the pregnancy, made an appointment at a women's health clinic, gotten dressed in one of those terrible paper gowns, gotten on the doctor's table, and put her feet in the gyno-stirrups hasn't thought about her pregnancy enough.[21]*

And as if feeling compelled to explain to pregnant women that abortions are abortions and fetuses are fetuses weren't bad enough, other legislation mandates outright lie to women. Informed consent laws in Texas and Mississippi require doctors to tell women that abortion and breast cancer are linked. The problem is, they *aren't*. Yet, despite studies and statements from highly regarded medical groups, like the National Cancer Institute, that refute any such connection, the virginity movement continues to promote this falsity in abstinence-only education, in its lobbying work, and now in five states' abortion legislation.[22] What better way to scare women than to tell them that a perfectly safe procedure could actually give them cancer?

Another kind of paternalism that's surfaced in the abortion debate is the idea that women who have abortions are victims—of the men who impregnated them, of abortion providers who are just in it for the money. From this standpoint, anyone is responsible—except the woman getting the abortion. This line of reasoning serves several purposes: First, it enables the woman-as-moral-child model that's so pervasive in virginity-movement thinking (and evident in informed consent laws). How can poor, unknowing women be blamed for medical procedures that they just can't mentally grasp? The other, more politically savvy purpose is that it allows anti-choice leaders and legislators to dodge questions about criminalizing women who have abortions.

---

* As anyone who has experienced an unplanned pregnancy can tell you, there's little else you *do* think about. The "deeper reflection" line is simply insulting.

After all, if abortion becomes illegal, then women who have abortions would go to prison. But anti-choice activists can't *say* that they want women to go to jail—most Americans would never support that. It's a political reality that they don't want to own up to.

In 2005, for example, a team of pro-choice activists filmed anti-abortion advocates trying to answer the question "If *Roe* were overturned, should women who have illegal abortions be punished?" If so, what should their punishment be?

The video made the rounds in the political and feminist blogosphere, gaining attention for the fact that *not one protestor* was able to answer these questions. They all cited women as "victims" of doctors, or simply said they had never thought about the question.[23]

In 2007, then–presidential hopeful Republican Mike Huckabee responded similarly to the question: "I think if a doctor knowingly took the life of an unborn child for money, and that's why he was doing it, yeah, I think you would, you would find some way to sanction that doctor. . . . I think you don't punish the woman, first of all, because it's not about . . . I consider her a victim, not a criminal."*[24]

By painting women as victims, the virginity movement doesn't have to deal with the political fallout—a lot less support for its cause—of saying that women who have abortions belong in prison.

It's also telling that Huckabee assumes abortion providers are men. (I suppose that makes it easier to portray them as taking advantage of poor widdle women.) Yet again, we're seeing the women-don't-realize-they're-getting-abortions-when-they-get-abortions argument in action.

---

* But of course, if *Roe* were overturned, she *would* be a criminal and *would* go to jail. It's an inconvenient fact the virginity movement likes to ignore in favor of describing scary abortion doctors who go *bump* in the night.

This kind of thinly veiled condescension is also evident in the earlier mentioned trend of pharmacists' refusing to give women contraception. The pharmacist assumes he* knows best, ignoring the decision made between a woman and her doctor. Not only is this invasive and presumptuous—it's also sometimes illegal.

For example, a pharmacist at Kmart, Dan Gransinger, wrote in an *Arizona Republic* letter to the editor in 2005 that pharmacists who take issue with dispensing EC should simply lie to their female customers:

> *The pharmacist should just tell the patient that he is out of the medication and can order it, but it will take a week to get here. The patient will be forced to go to another pharmacy because she has to take these medicines within 72 hours for them to be effective. Problem solved.*[25]

Something is amiss when a pharmacist can write to a local paper and unabashedly, and without fear of consequences, advocate breaking the law and lying to female customers.

One woman (who preferred not to be named, for fear of losing her job), a Wal-Mart pharmacy employee, emailed me to say that her supervising pharmacist refused to stock EC—a violation of store policy.

> *We are not allowed to order it, and if some comes in from the warehouse, he immediately arranges for it to be sent back. If someone calls asking for Plan B, we're supposed to say that we've run out of stock. This pharmacist apparently has NO problem dispensing birth control or Viagra, Cialis, or Levitra, however.*
> *[And] it's not just Plan B that pharmacists refuse to dispense. There have*

---

* I write "he" because I have yet to discover an example of a female pharmacist refusing to dispense contraception.

been two specific occasions that I can recall where women have brought in prescriptions for Cytotec and a pain pill, which is often used when women have had a miscarriage to pass any tissue that may be left. This pharmacist immediately began to question the doctor's prescription and whether it was being used to cause an abortion. In both instances, he wound up talking to the women about it, I guess so he could have a "clear conscience." One of the women had her young son with her, and she had to tell him to step aside so she could explain to the pharmacist that, yes, she had had a miscarriage and that was why the doctor had prescribed [Cytotec].

Shocking, indeed, but this kind of paternalism is par for the course in the virginity movement. Pharmacists for Life International, a group of extremist anti-choice pharmacists, are even *organizing* to make it easier to deny women contraceptives—and the ideology behind their actions is steeped in patronization. In a *Washington Post* article profiling the group, pharmacist Lloyd Duplantis said, "After researching the science behind steroidal contraceptives, I decided they could hurt the woman and possibly hurt her unborn child. I decided to opt out."*[26] The actual woman and what she wants are not even part of the equation—because, again, the assumption is that she can't make decisions for herself.

Behind all this paternalism is a simple distrust of women. The virginity movement doesn't just believe that women can't be trusted to make decisions about their bodies—it believes *men* can make those decisions better.

A group of legislators in Ohio, for example, proposed a bill in 2007 that would give men control of whether a woman could have an abortion. The bill

---

* It's worth nothing that the Pharmacists for Life website features anti-choice columnist Jill Stanek, who actually asserted that abortion providers and Chinese people eat fetuses! The group also calls Feministing a radical feminazi site, so I have a special place in my heart for it.

would prevent women from getting an abortion without a written note of consent from the father of the fetus. Permission slips aside, if a woman seeking an abortion didn't know who the father of the fetus is, she would *not be allowed* to obtain an abortion. In this particular legislation, distrust of women manifests itself even more clearly in the stipulation that women would be required to present a police report if they wanted to "prove" that the pregnancy was a result of rape or incest—because their word is not enough. (Not to mention, how does a young woman "prove" incest unless she reports her parent or relative—something that is too scary and prohibitive for many girls? That may be precisely the point.)[27] The bill is still being considered.

Similarly sexist attitudes are at play in "marriage promotion" programs—which some women have to attend in order to receive their welfare benefits.

In 2006, President Bush committed $500 million to the Healthy Marriage Initiative as part of the welfare-reform bill reauthorization. Instead of funding antipoverty measures that have proven successful—like education, childcare, and job training—this initiative supports programs (often religious) that tell women that marriage—not more education or a better-paying job—will save them from poverty. The idea is that women can't escape poverty on their own—best that they marry out of it. But, of course, many women in poverty marry men in a similar economic position.

And while the "healthy marriage" rhetoric sounds innocuous, its goal is most certainly not. This isn't about helping welfare recipients have "healthy" marriages; it's about ensuring that they have traditional marriages*—namely, marriages in which women don't work. Instead of encouraging a

---

* It's telling that President Bush cited his Healthy Marriage Initiative in the same breath in which he defined marriage as a heterosexual institution in a 2003 statement on the creation of Marriage Protection Week.[28]

two-income household, the classes teach women that it's better for them to stay home and support their husbands.

Given the promotion of family values that goes hand in hand with these programs, it's noteworthy that in 2004, one of the Bush administration's first marriage-promotion programs was charged with sex discrimination. The Pennsylvania-based marriage education course for unmarried couples with children offered employment services—but only to the men in the program. Another government-funded program, the biblically based Marriage Savers, makes the case that marriage is good for income because women can help men do better at their jobs by being, well, housewifely: "The married man won't go to work hungover, exhausted, or tardy because of fewer bachelor habits, and because he eats better and sees the doctor sooner, thanks to his wife. She is also a good adviser on career decisions, and relieves him of chores, so he can do a better job."[29]

Never mind that women are 40 percent more likely than men to be poor, and that 90 percent of welfare recipients are women. Better that we're married than given the opportunity to be educated and receive work training. Fear of women being unmarried—especially women with children—trumps logic when it comes to battling poverty. It's literally more important to the virginity movement that American women adhere to traditional gender and sex roles than that they are able to make a living wage. (Add common stereotypes about "welfare moms" with hordes of children, and it makes sense that these federally funded programs are so keen to marry off poor women.)

That's really what paternalistic policies come down to—what men want and what men think is best for women. And, sadly, too many of the men*

---

* Because, let's face it, considering the low number of women in political decision-making positions in the United States (women hold only 24 percent of elected state offices), it really is men who are formulating policy.[30]

who are making decisions about women and their health are very much invested in the purity myth, which tells them unmarried, sexually active women are bad, wrong, and in need of help, and allows them to create legislation that limits women's rights and opportunities with a clear conscience.

PURE PUNISHMENT

In 2007, while in Atlanta at the National Summit to Ensure the Health and Humanity of Pregnant and Birthing Women, I heard a story that forever changed the way I think about women, law, and punishment.

Laura Pemberton told a roomful of pro-choice activists, midwives, doulas, and feminist organizers how she was taken from her Florida home—while in active labor—shackled, and forced to undergo a cesarean section she did not want. Pemberton had wanted to have a vaginal home birth, but when she became dehydrated during labor, she decided to go to the hospital to receive fluids. When a doctor noticed a scar from a previous C-section, the hospital staff panicked—many doctors won't perform a vaginal delivery (VBAC) after a cesarean section. They told Pemberton that she wouldn't be able to give birth vaginally, and that she would have to stay at the hospital. She refused, and went home to continue her labor. (She actually had to sneak out of the hospital, as the staff had called the district attorney to come and compel her to get surgery.)

Once she was back at home, a sheriff came to her house, at which point her legs were shackled together and she was forced to go to the hospital, where a hearing was being held about the rights of the fetus—her child. A lawyer had been appointed to her unborn child, but not to Pemberton. After being *forced* to have surgery, Pemberton sued. She lost. The state told

Pemberton that her rights hadn't been violated; doctors could operate on her without her permission because the rights of her fetus—as defined by the state—trumped her own.*

I was particularly struck by this woman, who was devoutly religious and pro-life but had come to talk about her experience to a mostly pro-choice audience. "I was raped by the state," she said. She recognized that despite our political differences, all women are at risk under laws that dehumanize us and view us as little more than baby receptacles.

As horrible as Pemberton's experience was, she was luckier than others. In the early '90s in Washington, D.C., Angela Carder became critically sick with cancer. She was also twenty-five weeks pregnant. The hospital sought a court order forcing the twenty-seven-year-old Carder to undergo a C-section, in the hope that the fetus could be saved; despite medical testimony that the surgery could kill her, the court privileged the fetus's rights over Carder's own life. Carder's fetus, too undeveloped to be viable, died within two hours. Carder died within two days—the C-section was cited as a contributing factor in her death.[31]

These laws—the ones that express a fear of female sexuality and seek to control it—have one distressing commonality: punishment. This kind of legislation is punitive in and of itself, of course—whether it's criminalizing pregnant women who don't have healthy babies or shaming women who want abortions—but purity policies' consequences extend far beyond the language of a bill. Real women, like Pemberton and Carder, are suffering and dying because of laws that deem them less than full citizens.

The most recent law that epitomizes this principle is the federal ban on abortion. In 2007, the U.S. Supreme Court upheld the first-ever federal

---

* Pemberton went on to safely give birth vaginally to four more children.

law banning an abortion procedure.* The Supreme Court actually struck down the law as unconstitutional in the 2000 case *Stenberg v. Carhart,* in part because it made no allowance for women's health. But in 2007, when the court's makeup had changed, thanks to two Bush-appointed justices, women were not so lucky—the court upheld the ban. Justice Ruth Bader Ginsburg (currently the only woman on the Supreme Court) wrote in her dissent, "For the first time since *Roe,* the Court blesses a prohibition with no exception protecting a woman's health."

Of course, other purity punishments exist that aren't as dire as the ones outlined here, but they're disturbing all the same. Take the teacher who was fired for being unmarried and pregnant (a sin against the purity myth if there ever was one), or students at Liberty University in Virginia, who can be fined—yes, fined—$500 and expelled for having an abortion.† One legislator in Virginia even introduced a bill in 2005 that would make it a crime—punishable by a year in jail—for a woman to fail to report her miscarriage to the police within twelve hours.[32]#

So, you might ask, what does all this have to do with virginity: C-sections, abortion bans, miscarriage laws, and the FDA? Everything, really. The point of the purity myth is not only to valorize women who are "virgins," but also to prop up the idea of the perfect woman as a blank slate, as powerless,

---

* The law bans "partial-birth abortion," which is not a recognized medical term or procedure but refers to common abortion procedures used in a woman's second trimester. The legislation is written so vaguely that it could apply to any abortion (which is, of course, its intent). In fact, in 1998, doctors in Wisconsin stopped performing abortions pretty much overnight when the ban was enacted in their state, for fear of going to jail.[33]

† Incidentally, racial and sexual harassment costs them only $250.

Just in case you're unsure about how this one is related to purity, consider that the same lawmaker—who seems to have a penchant for legislation that involves women's bodies—is the man behind a bill that requires strippers to wear pasties.[34]

and in need of direction. Women who want to control their lives, especially their sexuality, don't adhere to the purity model. "Pure" women aren't just virgins—they're women who accept what extremist pharmacists tell them, who trust legislators over their own instincts, who don't question the notion that men should be in charge. In the past (as in the case of American female suffragists), women were told they shouldn't foul themselves by getting involved in the dirty business of politics. Likewise, women today are told to trust that their government knows what's best for them, their bodies, and their families. Power is not pure, so women shouldn't have it—and they should be punished for trying to obtain it.

CHAPTER 7

public punishments

"Rape, ladies and gentlemen, is not today what
rape was. Rape, when I was learning these
things, was the violation of a chaste woman,
against her will, by some party not her spouse."

SENATOR DOUG HENRY (D-TN),
2008

THE GANG RAPE OF a California teenager was caught on video: While
the sixteen-year-old was unconscious, she was raped vaginally and anally
with pool sticks, a Snapple bottle, and lit cigarettes while her three assailants
danced around her in between their assaults. At one point during the attack,
the girl urinated on herself. In her rapists' 2004 trial, the defense argued that
the girl was eager to make a porn video and was just "acting" for the camera.
The trial resulted in a hung jury.*[1]

A nineteen-year-old university student in Washington, D.C., after being drugged and sodomized in 2007, was denied treatment at local hospitals

---

* Thankfully, the second trial delivered guilty verdicts, but not before one of the boys was
arrested for raping another sixteen-year-old at a party held the night of his mistrial.

because she "appeared intoxicated"—not so surprising, given the nature of her attack. Even when the teen went to the police for help, she was turned away. Sergeant Ronald Reid, of the Metropolitan Police Department Sexual Assault Unit, was quoted as saying, "[I]f we don't have reason to believe a crime happened, we wouldn't administer a rape kit."[*2]

A year earlier, in Maryland, a state court ruled that once a woman consents to sex, she can't change her mind. Not if it hurts, not if her partner has become violent, not if she simply wants to stop. If she says yes once, nothing that happens afterward is rape.

Across the United States, a scourge of rape and violence against women is going unpunished and unnoticed. One in six women will be sexually assaulted in her lifetime; young women are *four times* more likely to be attacked.[3] But instead of these statistics' and these horrifying stories' being a national scandal, and instead of the media and government being up in arms over the epidemic of violence that women are facing, the reaction is largely silence—or, even worse, blame.

One would hope that the days of blaming the victim and qualifying what constitutes rape were long gone. But today, misdirected blame and rape apologism are even worse—because we should know better. More than thirty years ago, feminists fought to shine the national spotlight on violence against women. We've had access to books like Susan Brownmiller's *Against Our Will: Men, Women and Rape;* we've seen legislation passed, like the groundbreaking Violence Against Women Act, which allocated millions of dollars in funding to shelters and sexual assault services; we've watched *The Accused* and dozens of other movies and television shows about how rape isn't women's fault.

---

* The assumption in this case is that intoxicated women can't be assaulted.

But the myth of sexual purity still reigns supreme, and it grossly affects the way American society thinks about violence toward women. So long as women are supposed to be "pure," and so long as our morality is defined by our sexuality, sexualized violence against us will continue to be both accepted and expected.

INSTITUTIONALIZING BLAME

The Maryland law that a woman can't change her mind once she consents to sex was actually based on a case from 1980, which defined rape based on common law that considers women property (that's right—sadly, as recently as twenty-nine years ago, women were still considered the property of their husband or father). In this context, "rape" actually just means the initial "deflowering" of a woman; in fact, the injured party in a rape isn't even the woman—it's her father or husband. The decision notes that any act following penetration—the "initial infringement upon the responsible male's interest in a woman's sexual and reproductive functions"—can't constitute rape because "the damage is done" and the woman can never be "re-flowered."[4]

Not only is this a good reminder that a lot of laws on the books need a good updating, but it also demonstrates how directly notions about sexual purity affect the way violence against women is perceived, and even prosecuted. Women who have had sex can't be raped, because—as the law said—the "damage is done." They're no longer valuable; maybe they're no longer even women, in fact, but are completely dehumanized.

Devaluing women who have had sex is behind much of the institutionalized victim blaming that's so pervasive in America. The media in particular is one of the worst offenders; its coverage of violence against women gives us an uncomfortable glimpse into how widespread the purity myth actually is, and how it normalizes rape and violence.

The bulk of media response to sexual violence against women is mired in the stereotype of good girls and bad girls—rape victims worthy of sympathy and slutty girls who should have known better. The rape and murder of New York City college student Imette St. Guillen proves to be an interesting (though tragic) example of this trend, in that her story reflects both sides of the purity-influenced media coverage.

St. Guillen, a graduate student studying criminal justice, was out celebrating her birthday with a friend the night she was murdered. After her friend went home for the evening, St. Guillen decided to stay out longer and went to a local bar, the Falls. It was later discovered that Darryl Littlejohn, the Falls' bouncer, kidnapped, raped, tortured, and murdered the young woman.

The news coverage of St. Guillen's murder both sexified the story—referring to her as a young, beautiful woman who was brutally murdered*—and blamed her for being out drinking the night she was killed.

The initial, sensationalized headlines made much of St. Guillen's physical appearance: "Beautiful Co-ed Found Murdered," screamed the *New York Post,* calling her a "petite, raven-haired beauty."[5] The *New York Daily News'* headline was similar: "City beauty slain by beast: Tortured & dumped by road."[6]

But when the media found out that St. Guillen was killed after drinking alone at a bar late at night, the tone of the coverage changed considerably.

---

* Edgar Allan Poe once said (disturbingly), "The death of a beautiful woman is unquestionably the most poetical topic in the world." That quote always comes to mind when I see how the media unrelentingly plays out that narrative.

Now headlines read: "Slain Student Left Bar Alone After 4 am" and "Fearless in the city: Some women still party as if invulnerable."[7] The focus shifted from the murder investigation to (once again) girls gone wild—young women "putting themselves at risk*" by going out to bars and drinking.

Matt Lauer on NBC's *Today* show, for example, did a feature segment on the dangers of women going to bars:

> *Bars are usually safe spots to gather with friends. But the combination of alcohol and strangers can be dangerous, especially for young women. Cases like the murder of Imette St. Guillen and the disappearance of Natalee Holloway are important reminders that sometimes a night out can end tragically.*[8]

NBC sent a security specialist out to a bar to "find out how vulnerable women can be." CBS's *The Early Show* brought on former prosecutor Wendy Murphy and Atoosa Rubenstein, editor-in-chief of *Seventeen* magazine, to discuss St. Guillen and how women can stay safe. The conversation focused on girls' going out and drinking.

"But something like 85 percent of all crime has some connection to alcohol or drugs, so it's important as a matter of criminal policy-making that we talk about the role of alcohol and talk about drinking less," said Murphy.†[9]

St. Guillen's story is a textbook case of how concern can quickly turn to blame. One radio host, John DePetro of Boston's WRKO, said on his

---

* It's akin to women "getting themselves" raped. The actual perpetrator is rarely spoken of; it's another variation of "she was asking for it."

† Warnings about going to bars and drinking are rarely levied at men, despite the fact that in rape cases involving alcohol, it's often the *perpetrator* who has been drinking. Why not tell men not to get drunk so they don't rape?

morning talk show that St. Guillen's being out alone at 4:00 AM was "asking for trouble," and that women should use "common sense.

"As tragic as it is, your first reaction is she should not have been out alone at 3 or 4 . . . in the morning because look at what can happen," DePetro said.[10]

Wall Street Journal writer Naomi Schaefer Riley topped it all, however, when she penned a piece whose headline was . . . well, let's just call it transparent: "Ladies, You Should Know Better."[11]

Though Riley wrote that the murder was a tragedy, she made sure to point out that St. Guillen "was last seen in a bar, alone and drinking at 3 AM," and "that a twenty-four-year-old woman should know better." Riley went on to call women who drink and later get assaulted "moronic," and noted that if women wanted to avoid getting raped, they should simply "be wary of drunken house parties."

Of course, Riley's sentiment and victim blaming are nothing new. Author Katie Roiphe based her career on them. Her 1994 book, *The Morning After: Fear, Sex, and Feminism,* questioned whether date rape really exists and argued that women are in part responsible if they are forced into having sex after drinking or using drugs.[12]

> *Why aren't college women responsible for their own intake of alcohol or drugs? A man may give her drugs, but she herself decides to take them. If we assume that women are not all helpless and naive, then they should be held responsible for their choice to drink or take drugs. If a woman's "judgment is impaired" and she has sex, it isn't necessarily always the man's fault; it isn't necessarily always rape.[13]*

Let's face it—this is "she was asking for it" trussed up in language about agency and responsibility. Now, should we treat women as independent agents, responsible for themselves? Of course. But being responsible has nothing to do with being raped. Women don't get raped because they were drinking or took drugs. Women do not get raped because they weren't careful enough. Women get raped because *someone raped them*. Blogger Melissa McEwan, who wrote in 2007 about her own assault, said it best:

> *I was sober; hardly scantily clad (another phrase appearing once in the article). I was wearing sweatpants and an oversized t-shirt; I was at home; my sexual history was, literally, nonexistent—I was a virgin; I struggled; I said no. There have been times since when I have been walking home, alone, after a few drinks, wearing something that might have shown a bit of leg or cleavage, and I wasn't raped.* The difference was not in what I was doing. *The difference was the presence of a rapist.*[14]

Ah, yes, the *rapist*. Remember him?

RAPISTS GONE WILD

Victim blaming shrouded in empowerment rhetoric has become the norm when it comes to sexual assault and drinking—especially when assaults concern young women; to see this trend play out, you need look no further than the girls-gone-wild "trend," which the media is so very afraid of.

But rather than waste too much time on the media panic about girls' supposedly being promiscuous, let's talk about the *real* Girls Gone Wild—the company. The Girls Gone Wild (GGW) empire—a video and online porn business that brings in more than $40 million a year—is arguably one of the most blatantly sexually predatory groups in America today. Quite literally, it's a roving band of would-be rapists and assaulters who get treated like celebrities wherever they go.

The GGW crew travels from town to town, partnering with local bars and clubs to lure in young women who want to be on camera. And while many people still think GGW is primarily a Mardi Gras–type breast-flashing enterprise (which is certainly what it started out as), the company now deals in much more hardcore pornography. Though, of course, the story remains the same: The camera crew seeks drunk girls willing* to bare all, and maybe do a lot more, on video.

GGW's founder, Joe Francis, has incurred numerous rape and sexual assault allegations.† The most recent include a charge of misdemeanor sexual battery for groping an eighteen-year-old woman in California, a possible role in the 2004 drugging and rape of a college student in Miami Beach, Florida, and a community service sentence as part of a guilty plea for taping underage girls.[15]

But Francis is not a lone predator—the whole GGW family likes to get in on the fun, it seems. In 2006, a GGW cameraman was arrested for raping a seventeen-year-old Ohio girl in the back of the company's "party bus."[16] In 2008, video crew boss Matthew O'Sullivan, thirty-seven, was arrested for sexually assaulting a twenty-year-old Long Island woman—also on the party bus.[17] This isn't a coincidence—it's a strategy.

In an article about the Ohio rape, Carl Moss, an event coordinator who has worked with GGW on several occasions, noted that the company's staff acts in a distinctly "predatory" and "systematic" way.

---

* How willing these young women actually are is hard to determine. As you'll see in the following stories, their consent is often contested, and it's debatable how "willing" they can actually be to sign a legal contract when they're so sauced they can barely stand.
† And these are only the incidents that have been reported.

As the night progresses, the drunker the girls get, they'll start separat-
ing them. They'll say, "Hey, you guys want to come on the bus?" And the
girls'll say, "Yeah!" And they'll take three down to the bus. But when they
get to the bus, they'll say, "Well, we can only take one at a time because
you girls have to sign a release, and blah blah blah blah, and we'll come
and get the other two."[18]

The other girls will go back into the club, said Moss, while the cameraman takes a single girl to the back of the bus. "I've seen it every time now," he
said—as have others. The rape* of an eighteen-year-old girl by Francis, once
again on the bus, was actually detailed in a *Los Angeles Times* exposé on the
porn empire.

Eventually, [Jannel] Szyszka says, Francis told the cameraman to leave
and pushed her back on the bed, undid his jeans, and climbed on top of
her. "I told him it hurt, and he kept doing it. And I keep telling him it
hurts. I said, 'No' twice in the beginning, and during I started saying,
'Oh, my god, it hurts.' I kept telling him it hurt, but he kept going, and he
said he was sorry but kissed me so I wouldn't keep talking."[19]

Reporter Claire Hoffman, who also wrote about how Francis physically
assaulted *her* during their interview—pushing her up against the hood of a
car, twisting her arms behind her back until she cried—wrote that Francis's
lawyer, Michael Kerry Burke, responded to Szyszka's story by saying they had
had consensual sex, and "though Mr. Francis cannot speak to Ms. Szyszka's

---

* The young woman, as far as I know, did not press charges. But her description makes it
impossible for me to describe the incident as anything other than sexual assault.

discomfort during the encounter, other news stories have commented that Mr. Francis is reputedly well-endowed."*[20]

Despite these rape accusations, investigations, and unabashed physical assault of women, it's not Francis, his cohorts, or the company that get talked about when rape, drinking, and "going wild" are discussed in the media.† (In fact, they rarely get punished, either—you'd think that some of these men would be doing prison time, though none are.) It's women—portrayed as wild, sexual, irresponsible, and thoughtless. And little attention is devoted to the fact that these women are teenagers being systematically targeted by adults. Adults who have done this more than once. Adults who have the power of money, lawyers, and a society that loves to blame impure women backing them.

What's strikes me most about the GGW culture is that it's iconic in contemporary American society—these aren't just a bunch of frat guys who made a couple of bucks with a handheld camera. GGW is a way of life; it's a way of thinking about sex, sexuality, and women. Men, especially young men, look to GGW (and other pornography, as discussed in Chapter 4) for cues about what women are like—as sexual beings, people, and, ultimately, objects. As a result, our sexual paradigm centers on coercion, trickery, inebriation, and assault. And instead of screaming to the rafters that we're not going to take it, we wag our fingers at the young women who drunkenly take that trip to the back of the party bus.

---

* It takes a particular je ne sais quoi to make excuses for a rapist simply by noting how large his cock is.

† With the exception of pieces like Hoffman's, which revealed GGW's and Francis's true natures.

You don't need to "go wild" on camera to be blamed for an assault. Almost any woman can land in the "impure" camp and be blamed for sexual violence committed against her. "Impure" behavior isn't limited to being sexually active, either—drinking, staying out too late, or, in some cases, not being white all qualify as well.

Take Cassandra Hernandez, a female Air Force airperson who was raped by three of her colleagues at a party—where, yes, she was drinking. After she went to the hospital and filed a report, the Air Force treated her to a harsh interrogation—so harsh, in fact, that Hernandez decided not to testify against her attackers. Instead of giving her the treatment she deserved, the Air Force charged Hernandez with underage drinking and "indecent acts."* To make matters worse, Hernandez's three attackers were offered immunity from sexual assault if they testified against her on the indecent-acts charge. So, in effect, she was charged with her own rape.[21]

In the highly controversial Duke University rape case†—in which an African American woman accused three white lacrosse players of raping her—the media almost always referred to accuser Crystal Mangum as a "stripper" or "exotic dancer," despite the fact that she was also a college student, a mother, a *person*. The narrative became "stripper accuses college athletes," dehumanizing Mangum. In fact, the media was so enamored with this storyline that they expanded it to include *all* women

---

* The military definition of "indecent acts" is hard to come by, but the best one I found was a "form of immorality relating to sexual impurity which is not only grossly vulgar, obscene, and repugnant to common propriety, but tends to excite lust and deprave the morals with respect to sexual relations."[22]

† While the North Carolina attorney general declared the three men innocent, the aftermath of the accusation is ripe for analysis.

on college campuses. One ABC News article on the case reported on the "The 'Lacrosstitute' Factor":

> *They're on every college campus where sports teams succeed: groupies who want to date athletes—or at least have sex with them. . . . At Princeton University, where the men's lacrosse team is regularly ranked as one of the best in the nation, the women are known as "laxtitutes" or "lacrosstitutes."*[23]

Apparently, calling women whores isn't beneath even the most mainstream of media. And it's not just the press that uses women's sexuality against them when discussing sexual violence—it's the courts, too. In California, for example, a police officer who ejaculated on a woman he'd detained at a traffic stop—and threatened to arrest her if she took action against him—was let off even after admitting what he'd done. Why? Well, the victim was a stripper on her way home from work. In officer David Alex Park's 2007 trial, Park's defense attorney argued that the woman "got what she wanted," and that she was "an overtly sexual person."[24] The jury (composed of one woman and eleven men) found Park not guilty on all counts.

Similarly, a judge in Philadelphia ruled that a sex worker whom multiple men had raped at gunpoint hadn't been raped at all—she'd just been robbed. The victim, a twenty-year-old woman who worked for an escort service and obtained clients via Craigslist, had agreed to certain sexual acts with the defendant for a set amount of money. But he lured her to an abandoned piece of property and pulled a gun—then more men started showing up. When a fifth man was invited to assault her, he instead helped her get dressed and leave because he saw that she was crying. But municipal judge

Teresa Carr Deni insisted that what happened to this woman wasn't rape—it was "theft of services."

"I thought rape was a terrible trauma," Deni told a *Philadelphia Daily News* columnist. "[A case like this] minimizes true rape cases and demeans women who are really raped." Women who are *really* raped. You can't get much clearer than that—a sex worker just doesn't classify as one of these victims.[25]

But a woman need not be a sex worker to be blamed for her rape; having any sexual history at all can do the trick. Under the purity myth, the only women who can truly be raped are those who are chaste—and given how limiting the purity myth is, and how few women actually fit into its tight mold, the consequence is that *most* women are seen as incapable of being raped.

A woman who has had sex? Well, she's done it before, hasn't she? Not rapeable. A fat woman? She should be *happy* that someone would want to rape her.* Had a few too many beers? Take some responsibility for yourself!

This whole not-rapeable theme is especially true when it comes to women of color, who, as I've written previously, are either hypersexualized or dehumanized to the point that they're hardly even considered women, let alone "pure" women.

The rates of sexualized violence against women of color in the United States are far higher than those regarding white women. In fact, violence against white women is actually declining, while it continues to increase among women of color. Between 2003 and 2004, the incidents of intimate-partner violence involving black females increased from 3.8 to

---

* I'm sad to say this is a sentiment I've seen oft repeated in the blogosphere when women writers are attacked. The "rape as a compliment" theme never seems to get old.

6.6 victimizations per one thousand women. And the average annual rate of intimate-partner violence from 1993 to 2004 was highest for American Indian and Alaskan Native women—18.2 victimizations per one thousand women.

Naturally, it's not possible to prove that these increased rates of violence in particular communities are a direct result of society's positioning women of color as impure. But a society that portrays them as such absolutely contributes to a culture of violence against them—women who transgress purity norms are punished, and women of color transgress simply by not being white.

Again, all women who suffer under the purity myth are at risk—and the victim-blaming trend is extending far beyond only physical assaults. Women who are harassed—at work, on the street, or even online—are subject to the same rigid purity standards as women who are sexually assaulted. Just by virtue of being out in public, we're overstepping certain boundaries. (Consider how often a harassed woman is faulted for being on the wrong street at the wrong time of night, or told that she was too flirtatious in the office.)

But it makes sense; this is what the purity myth is all about. Pure women aren't out at bars or on the street; they're not in public life—they're home, where women should be.

While street and work harassment have been talked about for as long as feminists have fought back against them, disdain for women in public spaces has taken a new turn in today's tech-savvy world. The Internet is the new public space, and a similar trend is emerging there: Women who dare to transgress are being punished.

When women are harassed online—as they often are*—the excuse is

---

* A 2006 University of Maryland study showed that when an online user appears to be female, that person is twenty-five times more likely to experience harassment..

frequently of the "if you can't take the heat . . . " variety. When death and rape threats lodged against technology blogger Kathy Sierra came to light, for example, Daily Kos founder, progressive blogger Markos Moulitsas, said, "If they can't handle a little heat in their email inbox, then really, they should try another line of work."[26]

But women shouldn't have to, because the Internet is the new town square—it's a public place in the same way a street or a restaurant is, and harassment and violent threats there are just as damaging, maybe even more so. As I once wrote in an article about online misogyny for the *Guardian*, if someone calls you a slut on the street, it stings, but you can move on; if someone calls you a slut online, there's a public record of it for as long as the site exists.

When I was doing research for that article, feminist blogger Jill Filipovic told me, "There's a tendency to put the blame on the victims of stalking, harassment, or even sexual violence when the victim is a woman—and especially when she's a woman who has made herself public. . . . Public space has traditionally been reserved for men, and women are supposed to be quiet."

Indeed, something as simple as posting a photo online is enough to spark harassment and blame. For young women—many of whom have a public web profile, be it through a blog, MySpace, Facebook, or a Flickr page—this is a daily reality.

When Filipovic complained about harassment she endured from members of the law school forum* AutoAdmit, the site responded, "For a woman who has made 4,000 pictures of herself publicly available on Flickr, and who is a self-proclaimed feminist author of a widely disseminated blog, she has gotten pretty shy about overexposure."[27]

---

* Which involved talk about how they'd like to rape her, or their wondering how many abortions she'd had.

The mere act of having a presence—simply existing!—was enough for people to throw blame Filipovic's way. And with more than four in ten young Americans utilizing social-networking sites, and 86 percent using the Internet, Filipovic is hardly in the minority.[28]

A WORLD WITHOUT RAPE?

This intersection of women, violence, and purity has resulted in more than victim blaming and the idolization of predators like GGW—the purity myth is significantly changing the cultural and political landscape as it relates to violence and women. Women have always been blamed for sexual violence done to them; that's nothing new. But in an allegedly postfeminist world, where rape and domestic violence are supposed to be universally reviled, arguments that overtly (or stealthily) blame women, or dismiss violence against them, have that much more power. Because who in this day and age would say that rape is a *good* thing? Or that a woman just got what was coming to her? No one; instead, today's rape apologism comes wrapped in the rhetoric of equality—that's what makes it different, and so dangerous.

In a 2008 *Los Angeles Times* article, for example, reporter Heather Mac Donald wrote that there simply is no rape problem on college campuses. In response to a Harvard woman's story about being raped while she was drunk, Mac Donald wrote that to hold her "without responsibility requires stripping women of volition and moral agency."

> *Though the Harvard victim does not remember her actions, it's highly*
> *unlikely that she passed out upon arriving at the party and was dragged*
> *away like roadkill while other students looked on. Rather, she probably*

participated voluntarily in the usual prelude to intercourse, and probably even in intercourse itself, however woozily.[29]

This insidious argument about "responsibility" is having an acute effect on the way all women talk about rape. The very notion of what rape *is* is being debated—and not in a progressive or useful way.

Take *Cosmopolitan* magazine, which ran an article about a "new kind of date rape," written by none other than chastity pusher Laura Sessions Stepp (discussed in Chapter 2). What Sessions Stepp dubbed "gray rape" in her article is really just plain old terrible rape, laced with the same confusion and guilt that often accompanies an assault by someone the victim knows. But instead of taking it seriously and treating the issue with the gravitas it deserves, Sessions Stepp decided to water it down by naming it this sorta-rape:

> *It refers to sex that falls somewhere between consent and denial and is even more confusing than date rape because often both parties are unsure of who wanted what. . . . And it's a surprisingly common occurrence. The U.S. Department of Justice estimates that 1 in 5 college women will be raped at some point during a five-year college career; that about 9 out of 10 times, the victim will know her assailant; and that half of all victims will not call what happened rape.*[30]

Of course, *many* women don't call their assaults rape, for myriad reasons—perhaps because of the shame and stigma attached to sexual assault, or maybe they shy away from the word because they don't want to admit something so awful happened to them. But whatever the reason, it doesn't change the reality of what happened—it doesn't change the fact that someone raped them.

As dangerous as Sessions Stepp's claim that there is such a thing as "gray rape" is her insinuation that some women are too empowered to be victims. In the above-mentioned *Cosmo* article, she writes, "Even today, she is reluctant to call it rape because she thinks of herself as a strong and sexually independent woman, not a victim."[31]

Claims like these, and playing with language without regard for women's experiences, have real-life consequences. A young woman at Lewis & Clark College who was raped by a fellow student, for example, told a local reporter that she "calls what happened to her something akin to 'gray rape,' a term she learned from an article in *Cosmopolitan*."[32]

She relayed how she was "hooking up" with her eventual attacker when he forced her to perform oral sex on him.

> "I'm sitting up against the wall on his mattress, and he's standing over me," she said. "It started happening, and then he, like, twisted his fingers around my hair and started pulling it and being just kind of violent. I started choking because he was just, like, pushing my head. I started gagging and choking, and I couldn't really breathe.... And he was like, 'Yeah, that's right, choke on it.'"[33]

There is nothing gray about this. There is nothing gray about being violent. There is nothing gray about "choke on it."

But because this young woman read this one article—which was widely reported on by other large media outlets eager to glom on to a trend that says rape isn't really rape—her ability to name what happened to her was diminished. That's no small thing.

The language we use to talk about violence is quite literally being taken away from us. In 2004, a Nebraska judge barred the word "rape" from the trial of a man accused of . . . well, rape. The judge ruled that the language would be too prejudicial. The victim instead would have to use words like "intercourse" and "sex" to describe her attack.*[34] When this story first broke, Slate writer Dahlia Lithwick rightly wondered, "Is the word 'rape' truly more inflammatory to a jury than the word 'robbery'?"

The biggest indication of this regressive turn is the fact that the same people who are working so hard to blame women for their assaults, or to dismiss the fact that violence against women exists altogether, are also doing their best to fight against feminism.

Take Naomi Schaefer Riley, the *Wall Street Journal* reporter who wrote that Imette St. Guillen "should have known better." She not only blamed young women for their rapes, she also blamed feminism. In fact, her article's subhead was "How feminism wages war on common sense." Riley argued that feminism makes women think that they are equal to men (the horror) in all things, including drinking. She cited Barrett Seaman, author of *Binge,* who said that the college women he spoke to "saw drinking as a gender equity issue; they have as much right as the next guy to belly up to the bar."

"Radical feminists used to warn that men are evil and dangerous," Riley wrote. "But that message did not seem reconcilable with another core feminist notion—that women should be liberated from social constraints, especially those that require them to behave differently from men. So the first message was dropped and the second took over."[35]

Riley isn't the only one scapegoating feminists, of course. Mac

---

* In a heroic move (if you ask me), she refused to abide by the judge's rule: "I refuse to call it sex, or any other word that I'm . . . encouraged to say on the stand, because to me that's committing perjury. What happened to me was rape, it was not sex."

Donald and Roiphe took similar swipes, and it's quickly become a calling card in rape coverage. It's also at the heart of the larger conservative agenda. Conservative women's organizations like the Independent Women's Forum (IWF), for example, are quick to use the language of empowerment to enforce purity and dismiss rape, and thereby point the finger at feminism as "exaggerating" rape statistics or painting women as victims.

I've thought often about why—why?!—anyone, especially other women, would try to disrupt feminist work that combats violence. What in the world could be the point of that? The only reason I've come up with— and I think it makes sense—is fear of becoming that "impure" woman. Women who rail against feminism, like those at IWF, work hard to present themselves as "pure," whether it's through promoting abstinence-only education and decrying hookup culture or kowtowing to conservative men's agenda for women. It's a survival technique: If they can paint other women as "impure," then they're safe from criticism. It's a lot easier to attack other women, after all, than it is to attack a sexist society. Unfortunately, antifeminists are the only ones who benefit from their version of working on women's behalf; in reality, they put other women at risk and fail to solve any larger problems.

I truly believe that the drift toward blaming feminism is the most telling shift in this national dialogue. Blaming feminism, blaming *women's equality,* for rape reveals the crux of the issue. Because it's not concern that's driving media coverage of women's drinking too much—it's sexism. If it weren't, we'd be seeing dozens of news stories about the epidemic of young men binge drinking, blacking out, getting into fights, and raping women. But in our supposedly gender-equal world, pointing out these inconsistencies and double standards means ruining the utopian image Americans are so attached to. You're just whining—things are fine! Look how far women have come!

This is a lot to take in, I know: the idea that most of us—simply by living our lives, by being who we are—are at risk of being held accountable for violence against us. It's not a pleasant thought, but it's one we have to face head-on. The continual punishment and blame being heaped on women are unacceptable, and we can't sit silent as these patterns escalate.

beyond manliness

"The tragedy of machismo is that a
man is never quite man enough."
GERMAINE GREER

IN A COMMERCIAL FOR Milwaukee's Best beer, a group of friends is shown digging a hole in a nondescript back yard;* when a bee begins to buzz around them, one of the men starts waving his hands in fear and squeals in a high-pitched voice. As his friends look on in horror at this oh-so-unmanly display, a giant can of Milwaukee's Best beer falls from the sky and crushes the fearful man. A deep-voiced narrator says, "Men should act like men."

Other commercials in the beer company's "manly" campaign show men being crushed by cans for crying at the movies, talking baby talk to a girlfriend, and using a napkin to soak up grease from a slice of pizza. Milwaukee's Best's website features a similar "Act Like a Man" challenge: Once

---

* Because what could be more masculine than nonspecific yard work?

again, users are crushed by giant beer cans if they dance (the screen mockingly says, "That's some fancy footwork there, miss") or cry out in pain while getting a tattoo.

A Snickers commercial takes a slightly different approach (emphasis on "slightly"). An "effeminate" man who is speed walking—with a close-up on his shaking derriere—is quickly taught a lesson when '80s TV action star Mr. T comes busting out from behind a row of houses in a pickup truck, shooting Snickers bars out of a machine gun at him. All the time he's screaming, "You're a disgrace to the man race." The tagline? "Snickers: Get some nuts."

The message is clear: In order to be a man, one must avoid being feminine at all costs. In fact, the best way to be a man is to simply *not* be a woman. This oppositional definition of masculinity isn't limited to commercials, of course—it's everywhere. It's present in American politics: Male candidates pose in hunting pictures and denigrate their opponents as "girlie men." It's in pop culture: Television, movies, music, and, yes, commercials feature "real" men as those who shun femininity, and humiliating males is as simple as putting them in a dress or calling them Bambi. And, perhaps most of all, it's embedded in the myth of sexual purity, which is based on traditional gender roles in which men are "men," women are chaste, and a gender-based hierarchy is essential.

The fear of being feminine—something Stephen J. Ducat, author of *The Wimp Factor: Gender Gaps, Holy Wars, and the Politics of Anxious Masculinity,* calls "femiphobia"—is fundamental to America's current understanding of masculinity.

For many men, masculinity is a hard-won, yet precarious and brittle psychological achievement that must be constantly proven and defended.

While the external factors may appear to be that which is most threaten-
ing . . . the actual threat that many men experience is an unconscious,
internal one: the sense that they are not "real" men.[1]

Ducat, who is also a psychotherapist, credits femiphobia and male anxi-
ety about being appropriately "manly" to both our masculinized political climate and to some men's inability to sustain intimate relationships, and their
preoccupation with dominance therein.

"The problem is the psychological cost of developing a male identity in a culture that disparages the feminine and insists that the boundaries between masculine and feminine remain unambiguous and impermeable," Ducat writes.[2]

It's this psychological fear that makes so many men eager to bash the
feminine—whether that means making fun of feminine gay men, working
hard to prove their manliness, or simply bashing women themselves.

Julia Serano, author of *Whipping Girl: A Transsexual Woman on Sexism*
and the Scapegoating of Femininity, noted that this disdain for the feminine—
which, she says, is "regularly assigned negative connotations and meanings
in our society"—is far-reaching and deeply embedded in Americans' understanding of gender.

An example of this is the way that being in touch with and expressing
one's emotions is regularly derided in our society. While this trait has
virtually nothing to do with one's ability to reason or thinking logically,
in the public mind, being "emotional" has become synonymous with be-
ing "irrational." Another example is that certain pursuits and interests
that are considered feminine, such as gossiping or decorating, are often
characterized as "frivolous," while masculine preoccupations—even

those that serve solely recreational functions, such as sports—generally
escape such trivialization.[3]

In fact, women and femininity are so derided in American culture that it's not uncommon to see men punished via feminization. A prison in South Carolina, for example, disciplines sexually active inmates by dressing them in pink. Another Arizona prison mandates that all inmates wear pink underwear.[4] This shaming technique, however, isn't limited to convicts: A preschool in central Florida came under fire in 2004 when parents discovered that teachers were reprimanding unruly boys by forcing them to wear dresses, and in 2001, a teen sued his former school for forcing him to cross-dress (complete with wig and bra).[5] It seems that as far as punishment goes, nothing is worse than being a woman.*

And it's really women who end up being penalized because of these negative practices. This fear of women, this fear of being *like* women—even just a little bit—is at the heart of most misogyny in the United States. By fostering a culture that sees femininity and women as not just less than men, but also less than human, femiphobia is at the heart of enabling social sexism like the sexual double standard, political sexism that relies on paternalism in policy, and even violence against women.

MEN HURTING, HURTING MEN

In 2008, University of Connecticut student Melissa Bruen was sexually

---

* In my first book, *Full Frontal Feminism,* I opened by asking readers what the worst thing you can call a woman is (slut, bitch, whore, cunt), then what the worst thing you can call a man is (pussy, fag, sissy, girl). In both cases, the answers were some variation of "woman." I felt this bore repeating.

assaulted on campus while a group of male onlookers cheered. Even more troubling is that the assault was retribution for her fighting back against a man who had attacked her prior to her assault.

Bruen, who wrote about her ordeal in a campus newspaper, was walking home along a campus trail* when a strange man picked her up by her shoulders, pinned her up against a nearby pole, and started "dry humping" her. At first Bruen thought perhaps he was playing a joke on her—until she heard him moaning.

When she shoved the man, who was six inches taller than she was, off of her, he responded, "My, aren't we feisty tonight."

> When he came toward me, I grabbed him by the shoulders and pushed him down to the ground. I held onto his shoulders and climbed on top to straddle him. He started thrashing side to side, but I was able to hit him with a closed fist, full force, in the face.[6]

A crowd, mostly men, gathered—shocked that Bruen was fighting back. Her assailant got up and ran off, yelling at her. Bruen screamed at him and to the crowd, "You just assaulted me. . . . He just assaulted me." But instead of helping her, the group of men gathered in closer.

> Another man, around 6' 1", approached me and said, "You think that was assault?" and he pulled down my tube top, and grabbed my breasts. More men started to cheer. It didn't matter to the drunken mob that my breasts were being shown or fondled against my will. They were happy to see a topless girl all the same.[7]

---

* Not so funnily known as "the rape trail."

Eventually, Bruen broke free. What struck me about this story—other than the crowd's horrific, but not shocking, response—was that it's a perfect example of how women are punished for transgressing the gender norms that are so integral to the purity myth. Bruen, who presumably did what one *should* do when being attacked—fight back—was assaulted because, as she says, she was "breaking out of the mold" that expects women to be docile victims. Fighting back, after all, isn't ladylike—it isn't pure.

The same culture of masculinity that breeds femiphobia and the purity myth enables men to do near unimaginable amounts of violence to women (let's not forget Chapter 7) or, as in this case, cheer as violence is being committed. When women's sexuality is imagined to be passive or "dirty," it also means that men's sexuality is automatically positioned as aggressive and right—no matter what form it takes. And when one of the conditions of masculinity, a concept that is already so fragile in men's minds, is that men dissociate from women and prove their manliness through aggression, we're encouraging a culture of violence and sexuality that's detrimental to both men and women.

CRASHING THE GATE(KEEPERS)

If you want to see the purity myth in action, popular men's magazines and websites are a great place to look. (They're not always for the faint hearted, however.) For example, AskMen.com, an online men's magazine that claims to have seven million readers a month, published an article in 2008 titled "Training Your Girlfriend." It revealed perhaps a little too much about the way in which men are taught to view the women in their lives:

When you first start dating a new girlfriend, you want to be on your best behavior. Sure, you want to make a good impression, but what you're really doing is catering to her to get sex. The problem is, the power base shifts to her right from the outset and she knows it. She's in charge of access to the zipper and she counts on you bending over backward to gain entry. So she's got you.[8]

The piece goes on to "help" men get out from under the sexual thumb of women, using traditional dog-training tricks as a guide.*

The notion that women are the sexual gatekeepers and men the potential crashers is widespread not just in the virginity movement, but in mainstream American culture. The idea is that women are supposed to do all they can to limit men's access to female sexuality (and women themselves, really), and men are meant to do all they can to convince women otherwise. This sets up a sexual dynamic that assumes women don't want to have sex† and therefore need to be convinced to do so—and that this "convincing" is a natural part of seduction. But too often, underlying this model, what is called "seduction" is actually coercion.

Take a 2007 online article from *Details* that asked readers, "Is it OK to Demand Anal Sex?" In addition to having a jarring headline (when is it ever okay to demand *anything* sexually from a partner?), the article quoted men who had "convinced" women to have anal sex—which, according to the reporter, is more attractive than vaginal intercourse because "it's a harder-to-reach goal."[9]

---

* Notably, the article's author, Matthew Fitzgerald, also wrote a book called *Sex-Ploytation: How Women Use Their Bodies to Extort Money from Men*, available on Amazon.com for just $135. What a steal!

† And, as in all things purity related, women who do want to have sex are simply whores, worthy of derision and sometimes violence.

One young man, Josh, age thirty, told *Details*, "For most of my friends, it's sort of a domination thing... basically getting someone in a position where they're most vulnerable. But it's not like girls are ready for it—it's something they do when they're really drunk."[10]

Not "ready for it" speaks volumes. As does twenty-nine-year-old Albert's charming commentary on the subject: "Ideally, every girl is a disgusting pig who wants it."

Men's joy is in domination, a "harder-to-reach goal," and in giving women something they're not ready for*—and when women acquiesce, they're "disgusting pigs."†

Naturally, a selection of articles doesn't epitomize the full spectrum of straight men's sexual perspectives on women. But these pieces absolutely shed light on what is considered acceptable—and even lauded—male sexuality.

Author Michael Kimmel reveals in his book *Guyland: The Perilous World Where Boys Become Men* that this kind of sexuality—the point of which is to revel in dominance and "seduction," which can become predatory—is par for the course among young men. And it's not just what's defining their *sexuality*, it's what's defining them as *men*.[11]

> *The time-honored way for a guy to prove that he is a real man is to score with a woman. ... The problem, however, is that for guys, girls often feel like the primary obstacle to proving manhood. They are not nearly as compliant as guys say they would like them to be.*[12]

---

* Also known as rape.
† This message is not so far off from that of most abstinence-only education classes. The virginity movement positions men as sexual aggressors and women as ideally chaste, in order to keep supposedly uncontrollable male sexuality in check. And, of course, women who have sex are tainted. At the end of the day, it's the same idea, different mediums.

Kimmel paints a dark picture of young manhood in the United States, where porn is aplenty because it can't say no and where men will do anything to "convince" women to have sex—whether that means lying to her, trying to get her as drunk as possible, or even raping her.

One young man, Bill, tells Kimmel how he knows it's "not PC and all," but that he has pushed girls' heads down on him when he wants to receive oral sex, and that he once dragged a passed-out drunk woman to his room and had sex with her.

> *When she sort of came to a little bit, she was really upset and starting crying and asked why I had done that. I think I said something like, 'because you were so pretty' or some bullshit, but really it was because, well, because I was drunk and wanted to get laid. And she was, like, there.*[13]

What's more terrifying than the assault Bill perpetrated is the fact that he doesn't recognize it as such—he just thinks it wasn't "PC." But in an interview about *Guyland,* Kimmel clarified that he doesn't believe that this is what young men are naturally *like;* it's just what's expected of them: "As if guys are biologically programmed to be rapacious predatory beasts. I think that's 'male bashing'—and sets the bar far too low. I believe that guys can be men— ethical, responsible, and resilient. . . . "[14]

So do I. But while men's natures are being insulted by a code of masculinity that sees them as little more than walking dicks, it's women— like Bruen and Bill's victim—who are paying the bigger price.

What's more, positioning women as naturally nonsexual and men as innately ravenously sexual sets up not only a dangerous model that allows for sexual violence and disallows authentic female sexual expression, but also further enforces traditional gender roles—the main objective of the purity myth.

PURE MANLINESS

As much as the virginity movement is based on the idea that a woman's worth is dependent on her sexuality, it's also mired in the belief that traditional masculinity is superior and its preservation is necessary. In fact, the movement is so concerned about maintaining the masculinity status quo that it's staging an imaginary backlash. Organizations, pundits, and purity-pushing academics are up in arms about the supposed feminization and destruction of American men. And while a national crisis regarding masculinity is undoubtedly happening, it has nothing to do with feminization—hypermasculinity and femiphobia are hurting men. But questioning these norms means disrupting the gender power balance, something the virginity movement just won't have.

James Dobson, evangelical Christian leader and founder of the power-house organization Focus on the Family, is at the forefront of the movement to keep "masculinity" traditional. In fact, the entirety of Dobson's advice about raising boys, manliness, and fatherhood is that old-school norms about "boys will be boys" are part of the natural order—and he resents anything that calls that notion into question.

In his book *Bringing Up Boys,* Dobson drives the point home again and again that "boys are different from girls."*

---

* Dobson's derision regarding social change is palpable in his commentary immediately following that statement: "That fact was never in question for previous generations." These darn whippersnappers and their newfangled ideas about equality!

. . . Haven't you heard your parents and grandparents say with a smile, "Girls are made out of sugar and spice and everything nice, but boys are made of snakes and snails and puppy dog tails." It was said tongue-in-cheek, but people of all ages thought it was based on fact. "Boys will be boys," they said knowingly. They were right.

But Dobson's definition of what boys, and men, are is based completely in femiphobia and oppositional definitions. In a 2004 letter to Focus on the Family supporters, Dobson asked, "What does true masculinity look like?" His answer was "the physiological and emotional characteristics of a typical male are dramatically and intrinsically different than those of the typical female."[15] Men are simply un-women.* But he doesn't stop there. Manhood isn't simply about being different from women; it's about being *better* than they are.

In *Bringing Up Boys,* Dobson relays an anecdote about his son's "clearly identifying with [his] masculinity."

[A]s our family prepared to leave in the car, Ryan would say, "Hey, Dad. Us guys will get in the front seat and the girls will sit in the back." He wanted it known that he was a "guy" just like me. I was keenly aware that he was patterning his behavior and masculinity after mine. That's the way the system is supposed to work.[16]

It's no surprise then, that Dobson blames "radical feminism" for supposedly attacking traditional masculinity. And he's not alone. Other

---

* In fact, Dobson's fear of women and the feminine is so great that he often writes (in this book and elsewhere) that boys will potentially turn gay if they are not raised with appropriately masculine role models around them.

virginity-movement cohorts are also bemoaning its end and blaming its demise on the women's movement.

Kathleen Parker,* columnist and author of *Save the Males: Why Men Matter, Why Women Should Care,* for example, is certain that American men are in dire straits—they're mocked on television shows as bumbling dads and missing out on career opportunities because of "Take Your Daughter to Work Day." They don't live as long as women because of pesky programs that raise money for breast cancer, and are being increasingly feminized by an education system that won't just let "boys be boys." Parker's world is one where feminists, who keep insisting that men and women are equal,[†] have socially castrated men. (Naturally, Parker has an obligatory chapter on *The Vagina Monologues.*)

Her suggestion? "[A]cknowledge that men are not women and boys are not girls."[17] And, of course, put an end to the "radical feminism" that Parker believes is causing this gender confusion and male feminization.

Janice Shaw Crouse, of Concerned Women for America, agrees. She wrote in 2004, "[T]here is a concerted effort to mainstream the feminization of boys. We are familiar with the radical feminists' attempts to teach girls to act like the guys."[18]

Like Parker and Dobson, Crouse is concerned with maintaining gender norms: "[T]here is definitely nothing wrong with masculinity (boys being boys and men being men) or with femininity (girls being girls and women being women)."[19]

---

* You may remember Parker from Chapter 2: She's the *Washington Post* writer who fawned over Miriam Grossman's book and wrote that girls' having sex constitutes a "mental health crisis."

† Parker has also written that women in the military get raped by their fellow officers because "male soldiers and officers have . . . been forced to pretend that women are equals, and men know they're not." Quite a high price to pay for seeking equality.

Something about the fact that the language Crouse uses is nearly identical to Parker's and Dobson's is so telling—and so simplistic. None of these writers are making a real argument for a specific kind of masculinity, other than one that calls for men to not be like women. In fact, all of the people who claim to be so concerned about men's decline don't offer *anything* in the way of advice, outside of bashing women's social and political progress.

Take Harvey Mansfield, perhaps one of the best-known proponents of traditional masculinity and purveyor of feminization fear. A professor of government at Harvard University and author of *Manliness,** Mansfield argues that the decline of society—and of all-important manliness—is due to women's desire for equality and success outside of the domestic sphere, which he sees as disruptive to the gender binary system.

> *Women today want to be equal to men, equal in a way that makes them similar to, or virtually the same as, men. They do not want the sort of equality that might result from being superior at home if inferior at work. They have decided that work is better than home.[20]*

Women can't want to be like men, because that would mean that men are like women—a femiphobic's nightmare if there ever was one. And, like that of most purity-myth proponents, Mansfield's argument doesn't stop at women's engagement in the public sphere; it inevitably always comes back to the bedroom.

In all of the media and virginity-movement hoopla concerning girls'

---

* The original cover of the book featured the title scrawled across a brick wall. Apparently, the imagery was a bit *too* manly, so the publisher opted for an imageless cover instead. Ah, the bare aesthetic of manliness.

supposed promiscuity, one of the main talking points is a fear of women's "becoming like men" sexually. Mansfield, of course, is no exception. In a 2005 lecture, he blamed "radical feminism," which, he said, seeks to "lower women to the level of men" in terms of sexual behavior.[21]

"By the age of thirty, you see men who are used to getting free samples [of sex]," he said.

And like the men of Kimmel's *Guyland,* the men in Mansfield's world believe that women exist simply for male pleasure. In the same lecture, Mansfield noted that when "women play the men's game . . . they are bound to lose.

"Without modesty, there is no romance—it isn't so attractive or so erotic."*[22] (Why young women—to whom he is specifically referring—would care about what Mansfield thinks is "erotic" is beyond me.)

In order to please men like Mansfield, and to be accepted by women like Parker and Crouse, women need to be "women": passive, chaste, and accepting of male dominance and superiority.

So while virginity-movement operatives continue to promote the idea that men and masculinity are somehow in trouble, it's clear that what's really endangered are the patriarchal standards that they're so attached to. That's why feminism is *always* to blame. These books, articles, and arguments aren't a defense against an assault on masculinity—they're an offensive attack on progressive social change that allows women to be complex human beings, rather than purity-princess automatons.

---

* Indeed, Mansfield also noted in 2008, in an article about Sarah Palin, that "feminist women are unerotic." How disappointed feminists will be.

MOVING TOWARD A HEALTHY, SEXISM-FREE MASCULINITY

In his 2004 essay titled "Picture Perfect" author Douglas Rushkoff wrote about why he, as a young man, wanted to "go steady" with a girl: "It had nothing to do with her, really. Her purpose was merely to assert and define my masculinity.... She had only to prove I was not a fag."[23]

Women cannot continue to be the markers by which men measure their manliness. And while the myth of sexual purity is primarily about women, it's impossible to dismantle the notion that women's worth is connected to their sexuality without also dismantling a conception of masculinity that is reinforced so fully by that myth. We're only as pure or impure as men deem us to be—they're the ones with that power to define and control.

Masculinity and manhood need not be built on this foundation of sexism and gender binaries that the virginity movement is so desperate to hang on to. In fact, some American thinkers—including Kimmel and Robert Jensen (mentioned in Chapter 4)—dedicate their careers to this belief.

But the voices we're more likely to hear—those that appear in syndicated columns, control pop-culture mediums (like commercials), or run multimillion-dollar organizations—are the ones that continue to advance ideals about men and masculinity that are unhelpful, regressive, and dangerous.

Axe body spray (a noxious cologne whose lad-based marketing often peddles in sexism), for example, developed a TV ad campaign called "Nice Girls Gone Naughty." These commercials feature women becoming sexual predators, harassers, and rapists after smelling Axe spray; dressed as cheerleaders, nurses, and Girl Scouts, these "nice" girls appear in a lineup for having sexually assaulted the men in the commercials.

This campaign comes to mind because it trumpets what male sexuality is supposed to be—"naughty," aggressive, criminal—and turns it on its head. We're supposed to laugh and find the idea of women assaulting men hilarious (we're also supposed to be turned on by virginal girls gone horny for cheap body spray). But all this campaign does is use modern masculinity to make light of *actual* violence against women.

And this is why there's a real sense of urgency when it comes to doing something about the current state of masculinity. American culture recognizes that something is brewing when it comes to "manliness." It's a new antifeminist backlash of sorts, one that claims it's not about women at all, but about maintaining manhood. And whether it's an Axe or Snickers commercial, a book or an organization, other people are framing this conversation, and incorrectly.

It's difficult to question gender norms—especially perhaps for men, who simultaneously suffer *and* benefit from them. And I have no doubt that men suffer greatly under the model of masculinity that's ascribed to them; it's just not a natural state to enforce for anyone.

In an article called "The High Cost of Manliness," Robert Jensen outlines the restricting nature of what being a man today involves—a never-ending struggle for dominance.

> No one man created this system, and perhaps none of us, if given a choice, would choose it. But we live our lives in that system, and it deforms men, narrowing our emotional range and depth. It keeps us from the rich connections with others—not just with women and children, but other men—that make life meaningful but require vulnerability.[24]

It's because I care so much for the men in my life that I advocate a re-thinking of masculinity. It's also because I want a better world for women. Because as long as men are disconnected from women, as long as they're taught that we're what *not* to be, and as long as they believe that the only way to define themselves is through women's bodies and sexuality, the purity myth will live on.

Jensen calls for an end to our current understanding of masculinity. He says, "We men can settle for being men, or we can strive to be human beings."[25]

What's funny is that that statement essentially echoes the same hope I have for women: that we can start to see ourselves—and encourage men to see us—as more than just the sum of our sexual parts: not as virgins or whores, as mothers or girlfriends, or as existing only in relation to men, but as people with independent desires, hopes, and abilities. But I know that this can't happen so long as American culture continues to inundate us with gender-role messages that place everyone—men and women—in an unnatural hierarchical order that's impossible to maintain without strife. For women to move forward, and for men to break free, we need to overcome the masculinity status quo—together.

CHAPTER 9

sex, morals, and trusting women

> "If female sexuality is muted compared to that of men, then why must men the world over go to extreme lengths to control and contain it?"
>
> BARBARA SMUTS,
> *primatologist*

THE NATURE OF AN educational video produced by Concerned Women for America (CWA) is encapsulated in just the first few seconds, when the narrator says in a serene voice: "An honest talk about casual sex. False promises, searing pain, and tragic problems."

The video, of a talk that CWA's Janice Crouse delivered to college students in Washington, D.C., features Crouse talking about how promiscuity and hooking up are damaging young women. (She also relates a somewhat garbled history of the sexual revolution, which she says had "disastrous consequences for women.") Rambling off false statistics, Crouse tells her young audience that casual sex leads to poor grades, depression, and even suicide.

In 2008, the Clare Boothe Luce Policy Institute published a guide for college students, penned by none other than *Unprotected* author Miriam Grossman. *Sense & Sexuality: The College Girl's Guide to Real Protection in a Hooked-Up World* has a lacy pink design, and most of its text is cursive.*

Like Crouse's talk, the booklet features mostly scare tactics about premarital sex, including telling readers that the young men they have sex with are likely not to "remember your name," that "as the number of casual sex partners in the past year increased, so did signs of depression in college women," and that women who contract HPV† are essentially unlovable dropouts:

> *Natural reactions are shock, anger, and confusion. Who did I get this from, and when? Was he unfaithful? Who should I tell? And hardest of all: Who will want me now? These concerns can affect your mood, concentration, and sleep. They can deal a serious blow to your self-esteem. And to your GPA.*[1]

Not satisfied with simply telling young women not to have sex, Grossman also makes sure to lay on the pressure about early marriage and childbearing: "Remember that motherhood doesn't always happen when the time is right for you; there's a window of opportunity, then the window closes."

There's even a section in which Grossman seems to be wishing herpes on fictional characters. "It's easy to forget, but the characters on *Grey's Anatomy* and *Sex and the City* are not real," she writes. "In real life, Meredith and Carrie would have warts or herpes. They'd likely be on Prozac or Zoloft."[2]

It seems that no consequence, from herpes to suicide, is too weighty to pin on premarital sex.

---

* This sugar-and-spice presentation makes it particularly jarring when the following written-in-script statement takes up a whole pink page: "The rectum is an exit, not an entrance."
† More than 75 percent of sexually active adults will contract some strain of HPV at some point in their lives—that's an awful lot of "damaged" women!

In the world the virginity movement paints, girls are in grave danger—primarily from themselves. The "bad" ones are going wild, drinking, hooking up, and shunning traditional roles. The "good" ones are constantly at risk of being corrupted.

While there's no doubt that girls are in trouble—they're being targeted by a movement that's hell-bent on making sure they stay in "their place"—young women aren't putting themselves in danger. The people around them are doing the real damage.

Who? you might wonder. The abstinence teacher who tells her students that they'll go to jail if they have premarital sex. The well-funded organization that tells girls on college campuses that they should be looking for a husband, not taking women's studies classes. The judge who rules against a rape survivor because she didn't meet whatever standard for a victim he had in mind. The legislator who pushes a bill to limit young women's access to abortion because he doesn't think they're smart enough to make their own decisions. *These* are the people who are making the world a worse place—and a more dangerous one, at that—for girls and young women. We're just doing our best to live in it.

These people not only act in ways that have tangible consequences for individual women, they're also doing a great disservice to young women across the United States by participating in, and furthering, a culture that simply doesn't trust women. Whether it's about the decision to have (or not have) a child, the decision to have a drink at a bar late at night, or any number of daily life choices that people make, the virginity movement presupposes that women don't know what's best for them.

And when it comes to sex, the weapon of choice in the movement's push to deny women their rights, this distrust is amplified. Women can never make a choice about sex that is considered moral, or even acceptable, save for having straight sex within a marriage.* It's time to turn that around, for our own sake and for our daughters' futures.

DISTRESSING DAMSELS

There's a strategy behind talking about young women as out-of-control girls gone wild or innocent damsels in distress. If we're no more than sluts or victims, than it's reasonable for society to make our decisions for us—because, if left to our own devices, we'd muck it all up.

For those young women who are considered victims or potential victims—like the purity princesses or the young, white, suburban girls whose parents live in fear of MySpace stalkers and the corrupting influence of MTV—a "Daddy knows best" paternalism is omnipresent. Whether it manifests itself in the form of forcing girls to take virginity pledges and go to purity balls, or even is propagated by a casual joke when parents laugh about how they're going to have to lock their teen daughter away until she's twenty-one, the idea that these young women need protection spreads perpetually.

For the young women who don't fit into the perfect-virgin mold, the paternalism is still there, of course, but they also have to contend with the disdain that their "transgressions" incur. These are the young women of color who are considered promiscuous simply because they are not white, who are lesbians who will never fulfill a woman's "natural" role as a man's wife, or who are low-income and met with scorn when they choose to have

---

* And even then, women aren't safe from criticism—we're judged for having sex for pleasure and not for babies, for having sex that isn't vanilla, for being sexually voracious or less interested than our male partners. The pathology always lies with us, it seems.

children despite their socioeconomic circumstances. These are the women who are mistrusted most of all—so, instead of receiving paternalistic protection, they get punished.

In an article about Christian right members' opposition to the HPV vaccine, *Nation* columnist Katha Pollitt wrote that they "increasingly reveal their condescending view of women as moral children who need to be kept in line sexually by fear."[3] "Moral children" is *exactly* the right term. Whether we're grown women or young girls, the virginity movement assumes we're moral children—and American culture and politics treat us as such.

But this concept of women as moral children needs to be enforced consistently and pervasively for the gender power dynamic to remain as it is—especially now, when women are doing better than ever. And what better way to drive home the point that women are incapable than by shouting it in newspaper headlines and college talks, in legislation and the media? For virginity pushers and conservatives, there's an added benefit to framing young womanhood as a sexual disaster in need of intervention: It's an excellent distraction.

The fact is, focusing on hyped-up problems that sell newspapers and titillate the imagination make it that much easier to ignore *actual* problems young women are facing, issues that take a lot more than a moral scolding to fix. For a young woman living in poverty, spring break isn't even an option, let alone a concern. For a young woman who has no health insurance, the "moral" debate over STIs won't do anything for her the next time she needs to see a doctor. And for a young single mother, hearing about herself as an unfortunate statistic isn't going to make her life any better or easier.

If the same people who are working themselves into a purity panic over women's sexuality spent half as much time advocating on behalf of issues that young women really need help with, we might actually be getting somewhere. But instead, we're stuck talking about what a shame it is that young women are having sex, when the truth is, it isn't a shame at all.

GIRLS GONE NORMAL

The happy truth about young women and sexuality is that they're doing a lot better than all the "gone wild" hoopla would have us think. The stereotypical American girl, as pop culture, the media, and purity advocates imagine her, is self-conscious, not so smart, apathetic, and oversexed (think Paris Hilton and Jessica Simpson).

But a survey of five hundred thousand high school seniors from 1975 to 2005 showed that 70 percent of young women today report being happy with themselves, and that 77 percent are happy with their lives. The same study shows that 70 percent of young women think it's important to make a contribution to society, and that 90 percent hope to have a job that enables them to help others.[4] Young women are happy and think it's important to be socially engaged? Quite a different picture than the one certain conservative organizations and the media are painting.

Michael Males, a writer and senior researcher at the Center on Juvenile and Criminal Justice in California, dissected these statistics and others for an essay in the forthcoming anthology *Beating Up On Girls: Girls, Violence, Demonization and Denial.*[5]

Males reports that young women are smoking, drinking, and using drugs less today than in the past, and at older ages. He also debunks ever-pervasive hooking-up fears:

> [W]idespread claims by commentators of female sexual apocalypse are not borne

out. As far as I can determine, the damning term invented to label modern girls' relationships—"hooking up"—is meaningless . . . ranging from a casual email to an orgy. . . . If girls today are having random, unsafe sex by rising legions, we'd expect pregnancies and STIs to be rising as well. Again, just the opposite is the case.

But girls who are succeeding don't make for good headlines, and they certainly don't allow for the moral panic that facilitates the control the virginity movement would like to have over young women's lives.

Imagine how odd it would be to see magazine covers about the young women across the United States who are succeeding not only in school, but in life in general—making change in their communities and beyond. Young women who volunteer, young women who start organizations, young women who are activists—these women exist, but they're invisible in American culture.

The only time girls' success earns anything *close* to visibility is in the obligatory antifeminist articles about girls going to college at a higher rate than boys that argue that all this equality stuff is taking a toll on men. The only pieces about girls doing well are the ones written by people who seem to think that that's a problem.

Likewise, imagine how shocking—but wonderful—it would be to see statistics and media about how young women are making informed and safe sexual choices. Which—despite what we keep hearing—they are.*

Statistics show that sexually active young people are doing a lot better than purity advocates would have us think. Gone are the anecdotes about depression, falling grades, and shame. The real world of young sexuality is one in which young people are capable of making safe and

---

* Save for those who have had the misfortune of receiving abstinence-only education.

responsible decisions, which requires that we trust them enough to give them the information they need to do so.

It's no secret that a large percentage of teens in the United States—45.6 percent of high school students and 79.5 percent of college students—have had sex.

The good news is that despite the onslaught of abstinence-only education, cultural virginity fetishism, and slut shaming, teen pregnancy, abortion, and birth rates have dropped significantly in every age and racial group across the country. Between 1988 and 2004, the teen pregnancy rate decreased from 111 pregnancies to 72 pregnancies per one thousand teen girls.[6] And a 2007 study found that 86 percent of this decline could be attributed to increased contraception use.[7]

Advocates for Youth reports that sexually active teens are using contraception at higher rates, and more effectively: 70 percent of teen women and 69 percent of teen men reported using a condom the first time they had sex, and in 2005, 63 percent of sexually active youth reported using a condom the last time they had sex; these figures represent a 17 percent increase from 1991.[8]

The bad news is that despite these victories, the United States still has higher rates of teen pregnancy, abortion, and birth than other industrialized nations.[9] This problem is largely socioeconomic, as lower-income teens are more likely to get pregnant. In fact, nearly 60 percent of teen girls who have children are living in poverty, in part because poor teens are less likely to use or have access to contraception.

Statistics aside, the real question we should be asking ourselves isn't how we can stop teenagers from having sex, but how we can help them make informed, healthy decisions about their sexuality in general. And, perhaps more important, how we can foster a culture that values young women's ability to make those decisions.

TRUSTING WOMEN

Truth be told, I don't think there's anything wrong with the idea of teenagers having sex in and of itself.* I think sex is a good—nay, a great—thing, and that young people armed with accurate information are capable of deciding for themselves to have sex.

Sex—particularly as it pertains to young women—needs to be reframed as a moral and deliberate choice. Positioning unmarried, nonprocreative sexuality as dirty and immoral is not only dangerous but untrue. It's high time we trusted young people enough to tell them the truth about sex and sexuality: There's nothing wrong with them.

In this mess of chastity expectations, objectification, and control of women, we have lost a very fundamental truth: Sex is amazing, and there's nothing wrong or dirty or shameful or sinful about it. The virginity movement isn't the only faction that pathologizes sex; a mainstream culture that upholds the virgin/whore dichotomy and shames (or exalts) young women for their sexuality and little else has damaged sexuality just as much.

---

* I can already see the opposition taking this declaration and running with it, giddy that a feminist said she thinks teen sex is okay. Of everything I've written, this statement will get the most play. So let me be clear: I don't think that having sex is something that's "okay" for every teen (especially younger teens), nor do I think it's something that some adults are prepared for. I just believe that the decision to have sex has less to do with age than it does with being informed. I think that a sixteen-year-old who has had comprehensive sex education and who's been taught to have a healthy perspective on the emotional and physical responsibilities that come with sex is a lot more prepared for a sexual relationship than a twenty-one-year-old who has known only shame-based abstinence-only education and virginity pledges.

Teaching sex as a moral, responsible act—not to be taken lightly, but also not to be used as fodder for criticism—has the potential to create real change in young women's lives. By doing so, we'd be giving young women much needed space to take responsibility for their sexuality. For example, think of the common excuse that young people use when they've had unprotected sex: "It just happened." In these instances, sex is framed not as a deliberate choice, but rather as something that just occurred, thus freeing young people—especially young women—from the judgment that's heaped upon those who actively choose sex. The lack of protection, in fact, "proves" that the encounter wasn't premeditated; this allows the participants to absolve themselves of guilt. But if having sex is a morally neutral—or positive—act, young women will start making better and healthier decisions, because they'll feel justified in making them.

As it stands now, sexuality is still mired in the woman-as-gatekeeper model (discussed in Chapter 8), in which women are seen as, and expected to be, passive in terms of sex. This viewpoint not only negates women's active moral participation in sex, but also furthers a dangerous paradigm of men's feeling that they need to "get" sex from women.

Thomas Macaulay Millar, in the anthology *Yes Means Yes: Visions of Female Sexual Power & a World Without Rape,** asserts that sexuality in the United States currently follows a commodity model: "Sex is like a ticket; women have it and men try to get it."[10]

> *The commodity model assumes that when a woman has sex, she loses something of value. If she engages in too much sex, she will be left with nothing*

---

* Full disclosure: I'm the coeditor of the anthology, along with writer and activist Jaclyn Friedman.

of value. It further assumes that sex earlier in her history is more valuable than sex later. If she has a lot of sex early on, what she has left will not be something people will esteem highly.[11]

Millar suggests that we should strive to achieve a "performance" model of sex, which will not only rid our culture of the current model, which has done so much damage, but also promote a more woman-friendly ideal of sexuality, involving a moral and mutual decision-making process in which no one loses any "value."

Because it centers on collaboration, a performance model better fits the conventional feminist wisdom that consent is not the absence of "no," but affirmative participation. Who picks up a guitar and jams with a bassist who just stands there? Who dances with a partner who is just standing and staring? In the absence of affirmative participation, there is no collaboration.[12]

Millar's proposition is an incredibly important step in reframing the way we talk about sexuality—especially when it comes to young women. A Kaiser Family Foundation survey of young people found that 47 percent of teens who had experienced some form of sexual intimacy said they'd felt pressure to do something they didn't want to do—and young women were more likely to have had this experience than young men.[13]

While I believe wholeheartedly in young women's agency and ability to consent to sexual activity, there's no getting around the fact that society's current version of sexuality makes it difficult for young women to have a healthy sexual outlook that centers on their desires.

But unlike what purity proponents would have us do—push abstinence as the only appropriate option, and shame young women who choose otherwise—I believe that we should arm young women with the knowledge that sex should be a collaborative, pleasurable experience that has no bearing on whether they are ethical people.

Instead, the fact that sex is supposed to be pleasurable is often omitted from sex talks with teen girls.* Teenage girls' authentic desire—as opposed to the manufactured sexuality that's integral to Girls Gone Wild or to playing it up for guys—is a touchy subject for most. Young women's sexuality has become so disassociated from *actual* young women that it's tough to know how to begin reconnecting them with it.

We're living in a time when simply talking about women's pleasure is taboo in itself and is considered dangerous by the virginity movement, since that kind of discussion frees women's sexuality from its restrictive only-for-procreation, only-when-married, only-when-straight boundaries.

But when women's pleasure is being pathologized, it's imperative that we teach young women that there is nothing wrong with having sex because it feels good, that their desires and pleasure are important, and that sexuality should be—as Millar says—the presence of a "yes," not the absence of a "no."

I also believe in giving young women the room to explore sexually, and even make mistakes, without being judged. It's part of the learning process, and most of us have been through it.

A feminist backlash of sorts has taken place recently against the hypersexualized culture I've discussed in previous chapters—naturally, it's not just the virginity movement that takes issue with sexualizing girls and the mainstreaming of porn. Feminists, who have been speaking out against the sexual objectification of women since the '60s, have also been publicly debating this issue.

---

* Women's pleasure doesn't matter much. It's their "value" that counts.

Leading the charge against what she calls raunch culture is Ariel Levy, author of *Female Chauvinist Pigs*. Levy contends that young women participating in raunch culture do so by using "empowerment" as their excuse. They believe they're doing something feminist if they flash their breasts or have a faux-lesbian make-out session for a boy's benefit. Feminist Susan Brownmiller, author of the seminal book on rape *Against Our Will: Men, Women, and Rape*, said in Levy's book, "You think you're being brave, you think you're being sexy, you think you're *transcending* feminism. But that's bullshit."[14]

Levy's book is dead-on in many cases—when she discusses how raunch culture promotes inauthentic, performance-based female sexuality, for example—but she fails in that she seems to have little sympathy for the women she interviews, who she assumes are fooling themselves into thinking they're happy with what raunch culture has given them. And I'm sure in many cases, Levy is right. But I think we should give women a little more credit.

As reporter Kara Jesella wrote in 2005, "Participating in raunch culture may not always be a feminist act, but that doesn't make those engaging in it antifeminists—or deluded." She continues, "Levy rails against a culture in which 'the only alternative to enjoying *Playboy* is being 'uncomfortable' with or 'embarrassed' about your sexuality. But I know lots of women for whom there is a middle ground between rabid antiporn Dworkinizing and Girls Gone Wild vapidity."[15]

We should be giving young women some space to work out that middle ground—it's one way many young women come of age. Noted feminist Jennifer Baumgardner took on Levy's book in an article that asserted that though the new porned culture that further sexualizes women is a problem, telling young women they're being taken advantage of isn't necessarily the best way to effect change. A better approach, in Baumgardner's opinion, would be to own up to the fact that many women find their sexual footing through trial and error—and that there's nothing wrong with that.

> If pressed, I'd venture that at least half of my sexual experiences make me cringe when I think about them today. Taking top honors [are] the many times I made out with female friends in bars when I was in my early 20s. . . . I'm embarrassed about the kiss-around-the-circles, but if I didn't have those moments, I'm not sure I ever would have found my way to the real long-term relationship I have today. If all my sexual behavior had to be evolved and reciprocal and totally revolutionary before I had it, I'd never have had sex.[16]

Trusting women means also trusting them to find their way. This isn't to say, of course, that I think women's sexual choices are intrinsically "empowered" or "feminist." I just believe that in a world that values women so little, and so specifically for their sexuality, we should be giving them the benefit of the doubt. Because in this kind of hostile culture, trusting women is a radical act.

A PERFECT WORLD

Making sex moral and doing away with the myth of sexual purity are about more than trusting young women's sexual choices. They're about trusting women, period. Because if you can't trust women with sex, then you can't trust them with choices about family, about relationships, about anything. In a perfect world, our moral choices would not be seen through a filter that always includes sexuality.

IMAGINE A WORLD WHERE WOMEN'S SEXUALITY WAS SEEN AS NATURAL AND MORAL.

Natalie Angier, a science writer for *The New York Times,* wrote a wonderful book called *Woman: An Intimate Geography,* in which she discusses the myth that women are innately less sexual than men—a myth that the virginity movement often uses to its advantage: "Women are said to have lower sex drives than men, yet they are universally punished if they display evidence to the contrary—if they disobey their 'natural' inclination towards a stifled libido."[17] Women's sexuality and desire are natural, and we need to frame these concepts as morally sound if we want to free our daughters from the confines imposed on them now. As Angier writes, "How can we know what is 'natural' for us when we are treated as unnatural for wanting our lust, our freedom, the music of our bodies?" In a perfect world, women would be allowed to seek, and would be celebrated for seeking, that music.

IMAGINE A WORLD WHERE WE BELIEVE YOUNG WOMEN KNOW WHEN IT'S BEST FOR THEM TO HAVE A CHILD.

Whether we're attaching age-consent laws to abortion or imposing age limitations on birth control access, we don't trust young women to be able to control their own bodies. The truth is, most women—including young women—who choose to have abortions do so out of concern for their existing children, or for the children they'll have in the future. It's time to put to rest the stereotypes about women having abortions out of "convenience" or selfishness. Trusting young women means letting them make decisions about their bodies and their future, whether they're about access to emergency contraception, abortion, or even having children.*

IMAGINE A WORLD WHERE
TRUSTING YOUNG WOMEN MEANT
TRUSTING ALL YOUNG WOMEN.

In a perfect world, queer women's sexual and life choices would be seen as moral, too. Young women of color wouldn't be sexualized to the point of being dehumanized. Low-income women wouldn't be automatically misjudged as irresponsible. In a perfect world, these women would be seen as women—nothing less. The laws affecting women other than the perfect virgin are built on distrust: mandatory waiting periods for abortions that disproportionately affect low-income and rural women who can't take time off from work (or who need to travel long distances to get to their nearest provider); or the Hyde Amendment, which prevents federal Medicaid funding for abortion; or laws regarding violence against women that define some women as "acceptable" victims and others as asking for it just by existing. In a perfect world, all women would be trusted.

IMAGINE A WORLD WHERE
WE HAD THE MORAL HIGH GROUND.

For too long, we've ceded the language of morality to conservatives, and it's time we took it back. There is nothing morally upstanding about fetishizing young girls' virginity through abstinence-only education and purity balls. There is nothing moral about virginity pledges—just the opposite, in fact.

---

* Not to mention, let's be logical: If they're too young to decide to prevent or end a pregnancy, how are they not too young to have a child?

The purity myth relies on something George Lakoff calls "strict father morality," a paternalistic model of morality based in part on sexist hierarchies in which the "natural order" includes the idea that "men are naturally more powerful than women."

> *A traditional nuclear family with the father having primary responsibility for the well-being of the household. The mother has day-to-day responsibility for the care of the house and details of raising the children. But the father has primary responsibility for setting overall family policy, and the mother's job is to be supportive of the father and to help carry out the father's views on what should be done. Ideally, she respects his views and supports them.*[18]

The virginity movement relies on this framing of morality, but it's flawed—because at the center of "strict father morality" is the assumption that men, rather than women themselves, know what's best for women—and it's precisely what we need so desperately to turn around. (I'd call our new model of morality "wise mother morality" if it didn't reek so badly of cheesy goddess feminism!)

Imagine a world where moral turpitude for women was based on our making decisions for ourselves—not on our bodies, our sexuality, our skin color, or the number of sexual partners we've had. Imagine a world where women had nothing to be ashamed of.

Now imagine how we can make it happen.

CHAPTER 10
post-virgin world

> "For me, forgiveness and compassion are
> always linked: how do we hold people accountable
> for wrongdoing and yet at the same time remain
> in touch with their humanity enough to believe in
> their capacity to be transformed?"
> BELL HOOKS

ABSTINENCE CLASSES THAT tell girls they're dirty and used unless they "save it"; a culture that doesn't believe women who are raped; porn-based beauty standards for our genitals; a moral compass for young women that's based solely on sexuality. . . . There's no doubt that we have a difficult fight ahead of us, but I know we're up for it.

Taking on the purity myth, which is so entrenched in our culture, seems like an impossible task. After all, how can we simply "do away" with the notion of virginity? Even if virginity *doesn't* exist, try making that part of the mainstream conversation! How can we dismantle something as old and foundational as the virgin/whore complex? Sure, we can teach young people that the sexual double standard is wrong, but will they really hear it? And, of course, teaching young women to value themselves for something other than their sexuality is one thing; teaching society to wholly value young women is another story entirely.

The good news, however, is that challenging a culture that respects young women so little doesn't have to be a larger-than-life mission. We can chip away at it, bit by bit. Even better news is that a lot of Americans already are! They're organizing, blogging, getting together, and fighting back on many of the issues in this book. And you can, too.

CREATE MEDIA, GET ONLINE

The mainstream media is mammoth, but that doesn't mean we can't do something about the way it affects young women. Not only are existing watchdog organizations doing incredible work taking the mainstream media to task, but they're also creating new kinds of media that have a more positive view of women. And with the advent of the Internet, more and more everyday Americans are becoming citizen journalists and online activists.

For example, the hypersexualization of young women in the media—be it through fetishizing youth or running thousands of Girls Gone Wild stories that paint an inaccurate picture of young womanhood—is being addressed by organizations, blogs, and campaigns. Take New Moon Media, a girl-run organization that offers a positive magazine for girls, a blog, and action areas for girls and their parents; or WIMN's Voices, a group blog by almost fifty women who tackle media issues. (For a full list of blogs, see the Resources section at the end of the book.)

There's also the Real Hot 100 campaign—a project that aims to showcase young women's important work across the country and counter the negative image of young women in pop culture. Campaigns like this not only arm young women with a critical eye for unflattering media representations of them, but also highlight nonsexualized, positive images.

Such organizations aren't the only groups doing this important work. People all over the United States are making a difference simply by getting on their computers. One of the great things about the Internet is that we all have the opportunity to be media makers. According to one recent survey, there were more than 22.6 million bloggers in the United States in 2007, and more than 94 million blog readers.[1]

These blogs are opening up the Internet to more and more voices and opinions—voices that perhaps otherwise wouldn't be heard. Just look at the feminist blogosphere; ten years ago, if a woman wanted to be a prominent feminist voice, she had to be part of an elite national organization based in New York City or Washington, D.C. Now all she needs is a laptop!

Countering the conventional wisdom about bloggers—that we're just snarky writers*—is a tremendous amount of activism in the blog world. We're not just engaging in media criticism and news analysis—we're highlighting the work of local organizations, encouraging readers to participate in "real-life" actions, and proposing ways (from writing letters to sexist companies to developing bigger, theoretical ideas) to change a culture that so disdains women. (We're even affecting legislation—see the "Affect Legislation" section below for more on this topic.)

And the wonderful thing about using the blogosphere for media activism is that users can choose their level of engagement—you don't have to be a blogger to get involved in that world. Perhaps you're interested in women's rights. You can simply inform yourself by reading different blogs that cover the issues you care about, but you can also join in on the conversation by

---

* Okay, some of us *are*.

writing in the comments section or sending the blog to your friends. If you're ready to take even more action, you can start your own blog. Some sites, like Feministing.com, even allow you start your blog on their community site so you have a built-in readership. Any way you cut it, there are myriad ways you can participate.

GET ORGANIZING, GET EDUCATING

Creating new media and getting online are just two pieces of the larger struggle. We have to get more organized—because the virginity movement is not only well funded but also extremely well organized. As I wrote in Chapter 5, we are making strides against abstinence-only education—states are refusing funding and making comprehensive sex education a priority—but that doesn't mean we're out of the woods. In October 2008, Congress voted to extend funding for the Community-Based Abstinence Education Program (CBAE) through September 2009, which means, among other disturbing things, that crisis pregnancy centers across the country will get hundreds of thousands of dollars to continue to lie to women.[2] And state funding aside, the virginity movement is far from giving up on its most successful venture.

In addition to launching more nationwide campaigns through nonprofit organizations, purity advocates are also (smartly) rebranding their image. Perhaps recognizing that leaders like Leslie Unruh, known for being eccentric and extremist, were hurting their message, they decided to go more "mainstream." For example, the Medical Institute (formerly known as the Medical Institute of Sexual Health), which receives government funding, touts itself as a credible medical organization: Its website claims, "MI was founded to confront the global epidemics of teen pregnancy and sexually transmitted infections (STIs). We identify and evaluate scientific information on sexual health and promote healthy sexual decisions and behaviors by communicating credible scientific information."[3] Sounds pretty good, but the Medical Institute is in fact an abstinence-only organization that spreads false statistics about contraception; it even got funding to teach abstinence-only education to medical students. The movement is sneaking toward the mainstream, meaning we have to be that much more vigilant in our organizing.

It's not enough just to pay attention to the news and blogs and take action when abstinence education is up for refunding; we have to be more proactive. For example, ACLU's Take Issue, Take Charge website lists different ways for you to get involved, as does SIECUS, which has a community action site.[4] We can advocate for comprehensive sex education in our communities, our states, and even on the national level; and, most important, we can encourage our kids to get informed and get involved in their schools. Just an example: Tori Shoemaker and Cheyenne Byrd, two eighth graders in St. Louis, protested their school's abstinence-only education program by wearing shirts to school that were adorned with condoms spelling out SAFE SEX OR NO SEX. They were suspended for two days for acting out, but their story got national media attention and they got to be local safe-sex heroes!

Taking action can also be as easy as educating the people in your life about the issues you care about. Take the sexualization of girls, for example. In Durham's *The Lolita Effect,* she offers readers "strategies for resistance" that I think are incredibly useful, and not just for parents—they're for anyone who cares about the ways in which young women are sexualized. Durham encourages giving young people tools to assess pop culture critically, including media-literacy education—which she believes should be a required part of K–12 curricula—and encouraging creativity in girls by giving them outlets, like creating a website or a project that combats sexualized images. Durham also proposes increased consumer action, like sending emails to corporations. These are all great ways to fight back against the purity myth, one issue at a time.

Education is a key part of stopping the epidemic of violence against women. However, in addition to educating women and taking legislators to task, we also must talk to men and boys about ending violence against women. Organizations like Men Against Violence Against Women[5] and Stop Violence[6] are a great place to get info and tips for educating the men in your life.

AFFECT LEGISLATION

There are too many horrid laws on the books, or in the works, for us not to focus some energy on changing legislation and policy. You can follow legislation that affects women by being a regular blog reader or by signing up for action alerts from organizations like the Family Violence Prevention Fund, NOW, or NARAL Pro-Choice America. (For a full list of blogs and organizations, see the Resources section.)

The truth is, we can make a difference when it comes to legislation. In 2005, a Virginia lawmaker named John Cosgrove proposed a bill requiring women who miscarry to either report the miscarriage to a local law enforcement agency or go to jail for failure to report a death—a crime punishable by prison time. Word of the bill spread through the blogosphere, and the outcry was so intense that he withdrew the bill within weeks—and he actually credited blogs as the reason *why* he retracted it.

We should also be on the lookout for positive legislation that impacts women, like VAWA, the Lilly Ledbetter Fair Pay Act, or the Equity in Prescription Insurance and Contraceptive Coverage Act. This is about more than stopping the laws that hurt us—we must also fight for the ones that level the playing field!

SUPPORT LOCAL ORGANIZING

I'm a big believer in the idea that the most radical and cutting-edge organizing happens on a local level, and through smaller, lesser-known organizations and activists. Unfortunately, these are the people who don't get nearly enough media attention or funding. By focusing on supporting local groups and the actions in our community, we can help dismantle the purity myth from the ground up.

Reproductive-rights and health issues are a great example of where to start. Legislating sexuality and purity is wrong—whether it involves limiting women's access to abortion, telling them they *can't* have children, or enforcing traditional gender roles through policy. Women know what's best for themselves and their families, and our laws must demonstrate trust in them. The anti-choice movement—which doesn't just want to end access to abortion, but also seeks to stop women from obtaining birth control, from having children when and how they want to, and believes all premarital sex is wrong—is strong in numbers, funding, and political connections.

So we must support the organizations that are doing the important work of protecting women's reproductive health and enforcing justice. Yes, we should support organizations like the ones we know—Planned Parenthood and NARAL. But it's also crucial that we don't overlook the community organizing going on in our back yards, like the South Dakota Campaign for Healthy Families, or National Advocates for Pregnant Women.

Countless local women's shelters and health clinics are barely surviving. Find out who's serving women in your community, and help them do their incredibly important work.

GET PROACTIVELY INFORMED

A lot of the issues surrounding the purity myth are contentious, so make sure to become as informed as you can. Don't just wait for news to come across your desk; go and find out what the latest is on issues affecting the virginity movement.

For example, it's no secret that a tremendous amount of tension exists in the feminist community surrounding pornography. For some feminists, there's no such thing as woman-friendly porn; for others, the issue is more complex. No matter what your position on porn is, the key to changing the mainstream porn culture that denigrates women is to look to feminists involved in sex work and porn for guidance—feminists like Susie Bright and Tristan Taormino and Annie Sprinkle; feminists whose vision of sexuality and porn is diverse and thoughtful, like *SMUT,* a Toronto-based, queer, sex-positive magazine, or *$PREAD,* a magazine by and for sex workers.

And while feminists like Robert Jensen—whose work, discussed in Chapter 4, I respect deeply—would probably disagree with a lot of what these women have to say, I like to listen to *all* of them, because I think the answer is more conversation and more critique—not simple denunciation.

The purity myth is based on the idea that women are only as important as their ability to be chaste, and feminist porn turns that notion on its head. It lends subtlety and nuance to a narrative that the virginity movement and the mainstream porn industry alike posit as cut and dried. The most radical thing we can do to confront women's objectification and humiliation in some porn is to engage with it in a critical way. The same can be said of any issue surrounding the purity myth: We have to be proactively involved in educating ourselves before we take action on behalf of others.

DON'T GIVE UP!
FIND COMMUNITY, GET SUPPORT

When you're fighting against forces as powerful as the virginity movement, sexism, and misogyny, it's easy to get disheartened. That's why it's so important to find community and support wherever you can. And it's easier to find than you may think!

Groups like Drinking Liberally—which holds get-togethers at local bars for people interested in progressive politics—have chapters all over the country. The same goes for many feminist organizations, like NOW and the Younger Women's Task Force. And great websites like MeetUp[7] make finding a group near you that discusses the issues you care about as simple as typing in your zip code and area of interest.

And as I've written before (and will surely write again!), you shouldn't underestimate the wonderful communities available to you online. Whether it's on a blog, website, or forum, you can find people to share your stories with—your disappointments and your victories. A lot of women out there are interested in making change. Go find them!

Battling the myth of sexual purity and its consequences isn't just about trying to reverse the damage done to young women—we also need to move forward with a positive vision. That's why I chose a bell hooks quote to introduce this final chapter: We *must* believe in people's capacity to be transformed as we forge ahead, not only because hope is necessary, but also because it will allow us to do this hard work with open hearts and minds that will make our job easier. People *will* recognize that we're coming from a place of compassion and understanding. (Perhaps that's the optimist in me talking, but is there any other way to be when the cards are stacked so high against you?)

I wrote this book for the same reason that people around the country are doing this work: because we know that young women deserve better, and because we want a better life for our daughters. Too often, when a feminist—or anyone, really—asserts that American culture should have a more nuanced vision of women's sexuality, the virginity movement's knee-jerk reaction is to make the accusation that we actually want girls to be promiscuous, or that we think it's fine for children to have sex. It's a standard conservative talking point.

In fact, before this book was even published, I posted its cover image on Feministing.com and prompted an online backlash of sorts: Conservative blogs quite literally judged the book by its cover. A blogger for the Right Wing News wrote, "For them, it's not enough to say that, 'I'm not a virgin' or 'I like to sleep with a lot of guys,' they have to come up with some kind of justification for why it's the best way to live."[8] The Network of Enlightened Women, an antifeminist college organization, wrote on its blog that this book represents the alliance of the feminist movement "with the sexual liberation movement, although it wasn't necessary."[9] The House of Eratosthenes wrote, "Feminism, somehow, has come to be about everyone who can be a slut, being one."[10] Cassy Fiano posted that I must have an "obsession with sluttiness," and that the book's goal is to turn "teenage girls into raging whores."[11] Another woman, Ericka Andersen, even claimed to have read the book (despite the fact that it wasn't to be released for months!) and wrote that "the real purity myth is what Jessica is telling women: that sexual consequences be damned as long as you feel good."[12]

Now, of course, the book cover says nothing about sex, promiscuity, or "consequences be damned"—these writers made that jump. Why? Because for those who buy into the virginity movement, the only alternative to being a virgin is being a whore. There's no in-between for them; there are no shades of gray when it comes to sexuality, so they assume that if our intention is to attack the purity myth, our goal is to push young women toward promiscuity.*

So here's my challenge to the organizations and individuals who are working so hard to enforce the purity myth, and to roll back women's rights as part of that work: Be honest about what your goals are. Sure, you may think that traditional gender roles are what's best for society, but be up-front about the fact that those roles require women to be restricted in ways that men aren't in most regards. And please be honest about what this book, and work like it, are actually saying and doing. Don't fall back on hackneyed talking points about feminists' wanting girls to be slutty. Instead, try actually responding to the points we're making.

I have a similar challenge for those of us who are trying to dismantle the purity myth: Let us continue to tell the truth about what this myth means for young women, and to address our opponents not with derision and hate, but with understanding. Because for every person I've met who believes fully in

---

* For the record: I think virginity is fine, just as I think having sex is fine. I don't really care what women do sexually, and neither should you. In fact, that's the point. I believe that a young woman's decision to have sex, or not, shouldn't impact how she's seen as a moral actor.

the purity myth, I've met another who simply needed to hear the truth, compassionately and without their being judged, in order to break free from it.

And the fact is, we do have truth on our side: the truth that young women are suffering under this unrealistic model of sexuality and morals. And the truth that we are so much more than our ability to not have—or have—sex. We're more than virgins and whores. We're students, we're activists, we're parents, we're workers, we're people who care about the world around us.

We're women like Sandy Shin, a program coordinator at Breakthrough USA, an international human-rights organization that "uses media, education, and pop culture to promote values of dignity, equality, and justice." Shin was the legal advocate project director of the New York State Coalition Against Sexual Assault, and has long been involved with community-driven social movements.

We're women like Megan Kocher and Heather Ites, who own and help run Amazon Bookstore Cooperative in Minneapolis, the oldest independent feminist bookstore in North America.

We're women like Avideh Moussavian, the director of immigration policy and advocacy at the New York Immigration Coalition.

We're women like Jessica Yee, a youth activist who works on Native women's issues; or Deidra, who started the blog Black and Missing but not Forgotten, dedicated to all the missing black women, children, and men in America[13]; or Texas-based Noemi Martinez, who created the zine *Hermana Resist,* and who works by day as the human trafficking outreach coordinator at Texas Rio Grande Legal Aid.

These are the kinds of women who make up America—diverse, engaged, smart, interesting, *moral* agents of change. Take a look at the work these young women and others are doing. Now tell me it matters whether they're virgins or not (it doesn't), or that their contributions to society have anything to do with their sexuality (they don't). So let's use these examples of amazing young women to remind ourselves why we're fighting to end the purity myth—a myth that denies our value as whole human beings—and move forward with their work in mind. And let's spread this message about *all* young women across the country: that we're more than the sum of our sexual parts, that our ability to be moral and good people has to do with our kindness, compassion, and social engagement—not our bodies—and that we won't accept any less for any longer.

purity myth facts
at a glance

- There is no working medical definition for "virginity."

- "Vaginal rejuvenation"—in which a woman's labia is trimmed and her vagina tightened, or her hymen is completely replaced (a "re-virginization")—is the fastest-growing form of plastic surgery in the U.S.

- Over 1,400 federally funded Purity Balls, where young girls pledge their virginity to their fathers in a promlike event, were held in 2006 across the United States.

- Violence against women is going down, unless you're not white. Between 2003 and 2004, the incidents of intimate partner violence among black females increased from 3.8 to 6.6 victimizations per 1,000 women. And the average annual rate of intimate partner violence from 1993 to 2004 was highest for American Indian and Alaskan Native women—18.2 victimizations per 1,000 women.

- A 2007 report from the American Psychological Association found that nearly every form of media studied provided "ample evidence of the sexualization of women," and that most of that sexualization focused on young women.

- Over 80 percent of abstinence programs contain false or misleading information about sex and reproductive health, including retro gender stereotypes like: "A woman is far more attracted by a man's personality while a man is stimulated by sight. A man is usually less discriminating about those to whom he is physically attracted."

- Abstinence-only education programs, which cannot mention contraception unless to talk about failure rates, have received over $1.3 billion dollars since 1996, despite the fact that 82 percent of Americans support programs that teach students about different forms of contraception.

- Students who take virginity pledges are more likely to have oral and anal sex.

- Between 1995 and 2007, states enacted 557 anti-choice measures—43 in 2007 alone. Since President George W. Bush took office, state legislatures have considered more than 3700 anti-choice measures in total.

- FDA approval for Plan B, the morning after pill that prevents pregnancy, was held up after a FDA medical official wrote in an internal memo that over-the-counter status could cause "extreme promiscuous behaviors such as the medication taking on an 'urban legend' status that would lead adolescents to form sex-based cults centered around the use of Plan B."

- More and more laws are cropping up that attempt to curb pregnant women's rights, and even punish them. In 2004, a Utah woman was charged with murder after refusing to have a cesarean section and one of her twin babies was delivered stillborn. One legislator in Virginia even introduced a bill in 2005 that would make it a crime—one punishable by a year in jail—for a woman not to report her miscarriage to the police within 12 hours.

questions for discussion

- How do you define virginity? Where do you think this definition came from (i.e. society, parents, friends)?

- How do you think the ethics of passivity affected your life, or how do you see it play out around you?

- What values—other than "purity"—should we be instilling in young women to ensure that they grow up to be active moral agents?

- Were you brought up to think of female sexuality as somehow dirty? How did it affect you?

- How can we create a more positive vision of women's sexuality? What about younger women's sexuality—how can we do the same while not falling into the trap of sexualizing youth?

- How can we battle back against mainstream pornography that degrades women while still valuing women's sexuality and feminist expressions of it?

- Did you (or does your child) attend abstinence-only classes? What did you think?

- How can we get the word out in our communities and beyond that abstinence-only education teaches more than "don't have sex"— but sexist gender roles?

- How do you think the purity myth manifests itself in violence against women?

- In what ways can we use dismantling the purity myth to also fight back against rape culture?

- What do you think it means to "be a man"? Do you think that definition is useful, dangerous, etc.?

- How do you think masculinity contributes to the purity myth? How have you seen this play out in your own life?

- What are some tangible ways we change the culture of virginity fetish?

- Who are some young women in your life who counteract the current notion of apathetic, un-engaged youth?

- Imagine a world without "purity" and virginity. What does it look like?

notes

introduction

1. Jocelyne Zablit. "No sex please, we're daddy's little girls," *The Raw Story*, March 22, 2007.

2. PBS Online NewsHour. "South Dakota Abortion Ban," March 3, 2006, www.pbs.org/newshour.

CHAPTER 1
the cult of virginity

1. www.scarleteen.com

2. Laura M. Carpenter. *Virginity Lost: An Intimate Portrait of First Sexual Experiences* (New York: New York University Press, November 2005).

3. Laura M. Carpenter. Interview with the author, March 2008.

4. Dictionary.com definition of "virgin," http://dictionary.reference.com.

5. Hanne Blank. *Virgin: The Untouched History* (New York: Bloomsbury USA, 2007), 29.

6. Feministing.com. "Ivy Hymens: Why glorifying virginity is bad for women," March 31, 2008, www.feministing.com/archives/008913.html.

7. Randall Patterson. "Students of Virginity," *New York Times Magazine*, March 30, 2008.

8. Jill Filipovic. Response to "Chastity Clubs: Bringing the Hymens to Harvard Since 2001," *Feministe,* March 31, 2008, www.feministe.us/blog/archives/2008.

9. Advocates for Youth. "Myths & Facts about Sex Education," www.advocatesforyouth.org.

10. MTV. "True Life: I'm Celibate," July 2007, www.mtv.com/videos.

11. Denise Felder. "Miss America 'Purity Rule' Change Halted," September 14, 1999, www.ktvu.com/entertainment.

12. *New York Daily News.* "Miss USA Tara Conner Sex & Cocaine Shame," December 17, 2006, www.feministing.com/archives/006220.html.

13. Mark Coulton. "Trump deals disgraced Miss USA a new hand," *The Age,* December 21, 2006, www.theage.com.au/news.

14. Page Six. "Duck and Cover," *New York Post,* January 4, 2007, www.nypost.com/seven/01042007/gossip/pagesix/duck_and_cover_pagesix_.htm.

15. Fox News. "Miss Nevada Katie Rees Fired Over Raunchy Photos," December 22, 2006, www.foxnews.com.

16. Abstinence Clearinghouse. Online store, www.abstinence.net/store.

17. Feministing.com. "Shit . . . I'm out of petals," September 27, 2006, www.feministing.com/archives/005775.html.

18. Ultra Teen Choice. Abstinence Awareness Week advertisement, www.ultrateenchoice.org/.

19. Tyler LePard. "What Teenagers Learn (and Don't Learn) in Sex Ed," *RH Reality Check,* October 13, 2006, www.rhrealitycheck.org.

20. Sexuality Information and Education Council of the United States. "The Five Most Egregious Uses of Welfare's Title V Abstinence-Only-Until-Marriage-Funds."

21. Pure Love Club. Online store, www.chastity.com/store.

22. Carpenter. *Virginity Lost,* 40.

23. Love Matters. "Five Steps to Becoming a Secondary Virgin," www.lovematters.com/startover.htm.

24. Laurel Cornell. "Pure Again," www.focusonthefamily.com/lifechallenges.

25. A Pregnancy Resource Center of Northeast Ohio. "Take2 Renewed Virginity," www.pscstark.com/42.

26. Ibid.

27. www.modestyzone.net.

28. http://blogs.modestlyyours.net.

29. Janet Rosenbaum. "Reborn a Virgin: Adolescents' Retracting of Virginity Pledges and Sexual Histories," *American Journal of Public Health,* May 2, 2006.

30. Alexa: The Web Information Company. Web traffic data, www.alexa.com/data.

31. Centers for Disease Control and Prevention. 2008 National STD Prevention Conference press release, www.cdc.gov/stdconference/2008/media.

32. Feministing.com. "One more reason for comprehensive sex education," April 3, 2008, www.feministing.com/archives/008936.html.

33. Feministing.com. "If your hymen could be gift-wrapped, what would the bow look like?" December 28, 2007, www.feministing.com/archives/008311.html.

CHAPTER 2

tainted love

1. Camille Hahn. "Virgin Territory," *Ms.* magazine, fall 2004.

2. Laura Kipnis. *The Female Thing: Dirt, Sex, Envy, Vulnerability* (New York: Pantheon Books, 2006).

3. www.abstinence.net.

4. Ibid.

5. www.puriTeewear.com.

6. bell hooks. "Naked without shame: A counter-hegemonic body politic," in *Talking Visions: Multicultural Feminism in a Transnational Age,* ed. Ella Shohat (Cambridge, MA: MIT Press, 1998).

7. Ibid, 69.

8. Patricia Hill Collins. *Black Feminist Thought: Knowledge, Consciousness, and the Politics of Empowerment* (New York: Routledge, 2000), 134.

9. Education Portal. "Leaving Men Behind: Women Go to College in Ever-Greater Numbers," November 13, 2007, http://education-portal.com.

10. Via a Nexis search.

11. Mark Morford. "Bikini waxes for little girls—trend alert!," *San Francisco Chronicle,* April 11, 2008.

12. Cassandra Tognoni. "Giving out eye candy," *Daily Pennsylvanian,* October 29, 2007.

13. Kathleen Deveny and Raina Kelley. "Girls Gone Bad," *Newsweek,* August 21, 2007.

14. Lawrence Downes. "Middle School Girls Gone Wild," *The New York Times,* December 29, 2006.

15. Feministing.com. "A 'modest' appropriation of feminism," July 6, 2007, www.feministing.com/archives/007318.html.

16. Wendy Shalit. *Girls Gone Mild: Young Women Reclaim Self-Respect and Find It's Not Bad to Be Good* (New York: Random House, 2007), 10.

17. Physicians for Life. "Teen Sex, Depression, and Suicide," June 2003, www.physiciansforlife.org.

18. Shalit. *Girls Gone Mild,* 11.

19. Laura Sessions Stepp. *Unhooked: How Young Women Pursue Sex, Delay Love, and Lose at Both* (New York: Riverhead Books, 2007).

20. Ann Friedman. "Moral Panic Comes 'Unhooked,'" *American Prospect,* March 8, 2007.

21. Laura Sessions Stepp. "Cupid's Broken Arrow," *Washington Post,* May 7, 2006.

22. Miriam Grossman. "Shocked," *Town Hall,* March 17, 2008, www.townhall.com.

23. Kathleen Parker. "Dying to Date," November 16, 2007, www.townhall.com.

24. Ibid.

25. Feministing.com. "The child-like delusions of Dr. Eric Keroack," November 17, 2006, www.feministing.com/archives/006084.html.

26. Carol Platt Liebau. *Prude: How the Sex-Obsessed Culture Hurts Young Women (and America, Too!)* (New York: Center Street, 2007), 152.

27. http://dawneden.blogspot.com.

28. Dawn Eden. "Casual sex is a con: women just aren't like men," *Sunday Times,* January 14, 2007.

29. Carol Platt Liebau. "Girls Growing Wilder?" February 12, 2008, http://carolliebau.blogspot.com.

30. Carol Platt Liebau. "A 'Do-Me Feminist' Speaks," December 18, 2007, http://carol-liebau.blogspot.com.

31. Ethics and Public Policy Center. "Modest Proposals" conference announcement, www.eppc.org/conferences.

32. *Public Health Reports.* "Trends in Premarital Sex in the United States, 1954–2003," Jan/Feb 2007.

33. Laura Duberstein Lindberg et al. "Sexual Behavior of Single Adult American Women," *Perspectives on Sexual and Reproductive Health,* March 2008.

34. Guttmacher Institute. "Single Women Have Sex Too," March 11, 2008, www.guttmacher.org/media.

35. Guttmacher Institute. "Facts on American Teens' Sexual and Reproductive Health," September 2006, www.guttmacher.org/pubs/fb_ATSRH.html; John Santelli. "Explaining Recent Declines in Adolescent Pregnancy in the United States: The Contribution of Abstinence and Improved Contraceptive Use," *American Journal of Public Health,* 2006.

36. Advocates for Youth. "Decline in Teenage Pregnancy Rates Precedes Abstinence-Only-Until Marriage Funding," www.advocatesforyouth.org/factsfigures.

37. Centers for Disease Control and Prevention. "Adolescent Reproductive Health," www.cdc.gov/reproductivehealth.

38. Centers for Disease Control and Prevention. 2008 National STD Prevention Conference press release, www.cdc.gov/stdconference/2008/media.

39. Jacob Goldstein. "Teen STD Rates Cause for Concern, Not Panic," *Wall Street Journal,* March 11, 2008.

40. Yolanda Young. "Black teen STD rate needs our attention," *USA Today,* April 4, 2008, http://blogs.usatoday.com/oped.

41. Robert Fullilove et al. "An Epidemic No One Wants to Talk About," *Washington Post,* March 21, 2008.

CHAPTER 3

forever young

1. Feministing.com. "Padded bras for six-year-olds," September 11, 2006, www.feministing.com/archives/005685.html.

2. Feministing.com. "Who needs credit cards when you have a junior vagina?" December 11, 2007, www.feministing.com/archives/008226.html.

3. Cory Silverberg. "The 25 Sexiest Novels Ever Written," http://sexuality.about.com/od/eroticbooks.

4. M. Gigi Durham. *The Lolita Effect: The Media Sexualization of Young Girls and What We Can Do About It* (New York: Overlook Press, 2008).

5. M. Gigi Durham. Email interview with the author.

6. APA Task Force. Report on the sexualization of girls, 2007.

7. Ibid.

8. Generations of Light. "What is a Purity Ball?" www.generationsoflight.com.

9. Generations of Light. Purity pledge, www.generationsoflight.com.

10. Feministing.com. "Dating your parents: Not just for girls anymore," January 18, 2007, www.feministing.com/archives/006375.html.

11. Feministing.com. "Quick Video Hit: Purity Balls," October 24, 2007, www.feministing.com/archives/007972.html.

12. Pamela Jean. "Tell Me—What's So Wrong With A 'Purity Ball'?" *Digital Journal,* March 16, 2007, www.digitaljournal.com.

13. Jennifer Baumgardner. "Would you pledge your virginity to your father?" *Glamour* magazine, January 2007.

14. Lynne M. Thompson and Cheryl Gochnauer. "A Date With Dad," Focus on the Family, 2005.

15. Generations of Light. Testimonial, www.generationsoflight.com.

16. Judith Warner. "Pure Tyranny," *The New York Times,* June 12, 2008.

17. Ovetta Sampson. "Broadmoor formal aims to reinforce importance of father-daughter bond," *Gazette,* March 8, 2001.

18. Gary Cleland. "Tesco accused over padded bra for 7-year-olds," *Telegraph,* April 2008.

19. Charlotte Allen. "It's OK for Little Girls to Have Sex—As Long As They're Vaccinated," Independent Women's Forum, June 30, 2006, www.iwf.org/inkwell.

20. Katha Pollitt. "Virginity or Death!" *Nation,* May 12, 2005, www.thenation.com/doc.

21. Bill Maher. "Christians crusade against cancer vaccine," *Salon,* www.salon.com/opinion/feature/2007/03/02/hpv.

22. Rob Stein. "Vaccine for Girls Raises Thorny Issues," *Washington Post,* November 7, 2006.

23. http://blogs.modestlyyours.net/modestly_yours/2006/01/immunized_again.html www.parentspromotinginnocence.org/index.html.

24. Dr. Billy Goldberg and Mark Leyner. "Lost innocence or hormonal hazard?" The Body Odd, *MSNBC,* April 30, 2008, http://bodyodd.msnbc.msn.com.

25. American Society of Plastic Surgeons. "2000/2005/2006 National Plastic Surgery Statistics."

26. Laser Vaginal Rejuvenation Institute of New York. "Women Now Have Equal Sexuality Rights," *PR Web,* November 15, 2002, www.prweb.com.

27. Judith Graham. "Women urged to shun trendy plastic surgery," *Chicago Tribune,* August 31, 2007.

28. Kaiser Daily Women's Health Policy, Public Health & Education. "ACOG To Warn Against Vaginal Rejuvenation, Other Cosmetic Procedures," August 31, 2007.

29. Sandra Boodman. "Cosmetic Surgery's New Frontier," *Washington Post,* March 6, 2007.

30. Blank. *Virgin: The Untouched History,* 24.

31. Richard Estes. "The Commercial Sexual Exploitation of Children in the U.S., Canada and Mexico," University of Pennsylvania, 2001.

32. Girls Educational & Mentoring Services. Message from the director, www.gems-girls .org/message.html.

33. Rachel Lloyd. "From Victim to Survivor, From Survivor to Leader: The Importance of Leadership Programming and Opportunities for Commercially Sexually Exploited and Trafficked Young Women & Girls, Girls Educational & Mentoring Services, 2008, www .gems-girls.org.

34. Julia Scheeres. "Girl Model Sites Crossing Line?" *Wired* magazine, July 2001.

CHAPTER 4

the porn connection

1. Focus on the Family. "In what direction is the pornography industry moving these days?" http://family.custhelp.com.

2. Carmine Sarracino and Kevin Scott. *The Porning of America: The Rise of Porn Culture, What It Means, and Where We Go From Here* (Boston: Beacon Press, 2008), 12.

3. Robert Jensen. *Getting Off: Pornography and the End of Masculinity* (Cambridge, MA: South End Press, 2007).

4. Ibid., 80.

5. *Good* magazine. "Internet Porn: The Lucrative Business of Online Sex," May 2007.

6. Jensen. *Getting Off,* 4.

7. Ibid., 57.

8. Shauna Swartz. "XXX Offender," in *BitchFest,* ed. Lisa Jervis and Andi Zeisler (New York: Farrar, Straus, and Giroux, 2006), 318.

9. www.realdoll.com.

10. www.coverdoll.com.

11. Meghan Laslocky. "Just like a woman," *Salon,* October 11, 2005, www.salon.com.

12. www.sexdollrental.com. (As of publication, this site has been removed.)

13. MSNBC.com, "Sheen plays with dolls, destroys the evidence," October 10, 2007, www.msnbc.msn.com.

14. Ariel Levy. *Female Chauvinist Pigs: Women and the Rise of Raunch Culture* (New York: Free Press, 2005), 19.

15. Courtney Martin. *Perfect Girls, Starving Daughters: The Frightening New Normalcy of Hating Your Body* (New York: Free Press, 2007), 245.

16. Concerned Women for America. "'De-pornification?' CWA's Jan LaRue Challenges Young Adults," December 6, 2006, www.cwfa.org.

17. Brenda Zurita. "Score Two for the Perverts," Concerned Women for America press release, March 2008.

18. Barton Gellman. "Recruits Sought for Porn Squad," *Washington Post,* September 20, 2005.

19. Xeni Jardin. "FBI's new War on Porn—vagina, not Osama, is greater threat," *BoingBoing,* September 20, 2005, www.boingboing.net.

20. A Queer Tribe, "Obscenity Prosecutions," December 8, 2005, http://aqueertribe.tribe.net.

21. Associated Press, "Ala. sex-toy ban goes to Supreme Court," May 15, 2007.

22. Reuters, "Texas mom faces trial for selling sex toys," February 11, 2004.

23. Allison Kasic. "Take Back the Date," Independent Women's Forum, February 13, 2008, www.iwf.org/campus.

24. Clare Boothe Luce Policy Institute. "The Vagina Monologues Exposed: A Student's Guide to V-Day," 21.

25. Ibid., 23.

26. Lakshmi Chaudhry. "Babes in BushWorld: Raunch culture offers good old-fashioned pleasure, Republican style," *In These Times*, October 28, 2005.

27. Naomi Wolf. "The Porn Myth," *New York* magazine, October 20, 2003.

28. Andrea Rubenstein. "Sex-positive does *not* mean misogyny-friendly!" January 29, 2006, *Shrub*, http://blog.shrub.com/archives/tekanji.

29. Audacia Ray. *Naked on the Internet: Hookups, Downloads, and Cashing in on Internet Sexploration* (Berkeley, CA: Seal Press, 2007).

CHAPTER 5

classroom chastity

1. *Choosing the Best PATH*. Teachers' guide, 7.

2. Michael Alison Chandler. "Christian Sex-Ed Lesson Criticized," *Washington Post*, March 15, 2007.

3. Henry Waxman. "The Content of Federally Funded Abstinence-Only Education Programs," United States House of Representatives Committee on Government Reform, Special Investigations Division, December 2004.

4. Ibid., 13–14.

5. Ibid.

6. *Me, My World, My Future*. Revised HIV material, 258.

7. *Reasonable Reasons to Wait*. Teachers' guide (unit 5): 19.

8. *Sex Respect*. Student workbook, 11.

9. WAIT training.

10. *Choosing the Best Life*. Leader guide, 7.

11. http://proknowledge.org.

12. *Why kNOw*. Abstinence-only textbook, 59.

13. Ibid., 61.

14. *Reasonable Reasons to Wait*.

15. Friends First. WAIT training manual.

16. *Why kNOw*, 76.

17. U.S. Department of Health and Human Services, Administration on Children, Youth and Families. "Child Maltreatment 2004," Chapter 3, 2006.

18. No More Money. "Reality Behind Programs," 2005, www.nomoremoney.org/reality.html.

19. Administration for Children and Families (ACF) at the U.S. Department of Health and Human Services. New guidelines.

20. Nico Pitney, "New Bush Policy: All Gays Should Be Celibate," *Think Progress,* April 17, 2006, http://thinkprogress.org.

21. Zazzle. Online "Wait Wear" store, www.zazzle.com/waitwear.

22. Feministing.com. "No sex for you, my pretty!" May 31, 2006, www.feministing.com/archives/005129.html.

23. Abstinence Clearinghouse. Abstinence Idol registration, www.abstinenceconference.net.

24. John Santelli et al. "Abstinence and abstinence-only education: A review of U.S. policies and programs," *Journal of Adolescent Health* 38, no. 1 (2006): 72–81.

25. Karen Perrin. "Abstinence-Only Education: How We Got Here and Where We're Going," *Journal of Public Health Policy,* January 1, 2003.

26. Daley. "Exclusive Purpose," SIECUS report, April/May 1, 1997.

27. Perrin. "Abstinence-Only Education."

28. Title V, Section 510 of the Social Security Act.

29. Advocates for Youth. "The History of Federal Abstinence-Only Funding," www.advocatesforyouth.org/publications.

30. Legal Momentum. "Sex, Lies & Stereotypes: Profiles of Federally Abstinence-Only Grant Recipients," www.legalmomentum.org.

31. Feministing.com. "Leslee Unruh is coming for your babies," May 24, 2007, www.feministing.com/archives/007079.html.

32. Myra Batchelder, "Who Is Leslee Unruh?" Planned Parenthood, May 10, 2006, www.plannedparenthood.org/issues-action.

33. Eric Resnick, "State 'abstinence' head suspended in ethics case," *Gay People's Chronicle,* April 14, 2006, www.gaypeopleschronicle.com.

34. Legal Momentum. "Sex, Lies & Stereotypes: Profiles of Federally Funded Abstinence-Only Grant Recipients."

35. Ibid.

36. Amy Bleakley, PhD, MPH, Michael Hennessy, PhD, MPH, and Martin Fishbein, PhD. "Public Opinion on Sex Education in US Schools" *Pediatrics & Adolescent Medicine* 160 (2006):1151–1156.

37. Documentary Educational Resources. *Abstinence Comes to Albuquerque* website, www.der.org/films/abstinence-comes-to-albuquerque.html.

38. YouTube. "BULL$#!+ - Abstinence Only" video, www.youtube.com.

39. www.rhrealitycheck.org/blog/2007/04/09/abstinence-only-abstaining-from-ethics-while-imposing-morality.

40. American Psychological Association. "Based on the Research, Comprehensive Sex

Education Is More Effective at Stopping the Spread of HIV Infection, Says APA Committee," February 23, 2005, www.apa.org/releases/sexeducation.html; American Medical Association. "Sexuality Education, Abstinence, and Distribution of Condoms in Schools," www.ama-assn.org; American Academy of Pediatrics. "Sexuality Education for Children and Adolescents," *Pediatrics* 108 (2001): 498–502; American Public Health Association. "Abstinence and U.S. Abstinence-Only Education Policies: Ethical and Human Rights Concerns," www.apha.org/advocacy/policy.

41. Kevin Freking. "States Refuse Abstinence Ed. Grants," *Time,* June 24, 2008, www.time.com/time/politics.

42. www.parentsfortruth.org.

43. Rob Stein. "U.S. Campaign to Promote Abstinence Begins," *Washington Post,* June 1, 2008.

44. Christopher Trenholm, Barbara Devaney, et al. "Impacts of Four Title V, Section 510 Abstinence Education Programs," 2007.

45. Hannah Brückner and Peter Bearman. "After the promise: The STD consequences of adolescent virginity pledges," *Journal of Adolescent Health* 36, no. 4 (2005): 271–78.

CHAPTER 6

legislating sexuality

1. Archive of the Biting Beaver. "Morality causes, EC, and broken condoms," May 31, 2008, http://archiveofthebitingbeaver.wordpress.com.

2. NARAL Pro-Choice America. Refusal to Provide Medical Services, *Who Decides?,* 2007.

3. Cristina Page. Interview with the author, December 2008.

4. NARAL Pro-Choice America. *Who Decides?*

5. Jim Abrams. "30 states said at risk of abortion ban," Associated Press, October 6, 2004.

6. Lawrence B. Finer and Stanley K. Henshaw. "Abortion Incidence and Services in the United States in 2000," *Perspectives on Sexual and Reproductive Health,* January/February 2003.

7. Stanley K. Henshaw. "Abortion Incidence and Services in the United States, 1995–1996," *Family Planning Perspectives,* November/December 1998.

8. Katha Pollitt. "Pregnant and Dangerous," *Nation,* April 8, 2004; Rick Montgomery. "Push for fetal safety blurs women's rights," McClatchy Newspapers, July 11, 2006.

9. Montgomery. "Push for fetal safety."

10. January W. Payne. "Forever Pregnant," *Washington Post,* May 16, 2006.

11. Ann Friedman. "Over-the-Counter Insurgency," *Mother Jones,* August 1, 2006.

12. U.S. Food and Drug Administration. Meeting transcript, December 16, 2004, www.fda. gov/ohrms/dockets.

13. Gina Kolata. "A Contraceptive Clears a Hurdle to Wider Access," *The New York Times,* December 17, 2003.

14. David Hager. *Stress and the Woman's Body* (Ada, MI: Revell, 1998).

15. Kristina Shaw. "Protecting women's reproductive rights on college campuses," *Minnesota Daily,* July 27, 2005. Blog for Choice. "BC availability on campus 'outrages' Wisconsin lawmaker," March 18, 2005, www.blogforchoice.com.

16. Marc Kaufman. "9 Arrested Protesting Morning-After Pill Plan," *Washington Post,* January 8, 2005; Government Accountability Office. "Decision Process to Deny Initial Application for Over-the-Counter Marketing of the Emergency Contraceptive Drug Plan B Was Unusual," November 14, 2005, www.gao.gov/new.items/d06109.pdf.

17. Rachel Benson Gold and Elizabeth Nash. "State Abortion Counseling Policies and the Fundamental Principles of Informed Consent," *Guttmacher Policy Review* 10, no. 4 (2007).

18. South Dakota Legislature. South Dakota Codified Laws, http://legis.state.sd.us/ statutes.

19. Sarah Blustain. "Consenting Adults," *American Prospect*, April 13, 2007.

20. The Guttmacher Institute. State policies in brief, October 2008.

21. Eric Kleefeld. "Brownback Would Require Women To Get An Ultrasound Before An Abortion," TPM Election Central, September 20, 2007.

22. Chinué Turner Richardson and Elizabeth Nash. "Misinformed Consent: The Medical Accuracy of State-Developed Abortion Counseling Materials," *Guttmacher Policy Review* 9, no. 4 (2006).

23. At Center Network. Libertyville abortion demonstration video, www.atcenternetwork. com/?p=64.

24. John Solomon. "Huckabee Would Criminalize Abortion Providers," The Trail, *Washington Post,* December 30, 2007.

25. NARAL Pro-Choice Arizona. "NARAL Pro-Choice Arizona asks K-mart to take action against pharmacist manager who counseled lying about availability of birth control," April 26, 2005.

26. Rob Stein. "'Pro-Life' Drugstores Market Beliefs," *Washington Post,* June 16, 2008.

27. Mike Hixenbaugh. "Abortion law would give fathers a say State legislators propose change," *Record-Courier,* July 30, 2007.

28. George W. Bush. "Marriage Protection Week, 2003: A Proclamation," October 3, 2003, www.whitehouse.gov/news.

29. Jessica Valenti. "A Good Job Is Hard to Find," *AlterNet,* April 5, 2006.

30. Rutgers Center for American Woman and Politics. Fast Facts: Levels of Office, www
.cawp.rutgers.edu/fast_facts/levels_of_office.

31. Lynn M. Paltrow and TomPaine.com. "Coercive Medicine," National Advocates for
Pregnant Women, March 21, 2004, http://advocatesforpregnantwomen.org/main/
publications.

32. Center for Reproductive Rights. "The NYT Criticizes 'Partial-Birth' Strategy," *Reproductive Freedom News* VII, no. 5 (1998).

33. Daily Kos. "VA Legislative Sentry: Have a Miscarriage, Go to JAIL?" January 6, 2005,
www.dailykos.com.

34. Feministing.com. "A loser legislator makes his big comeback," March 18, 2008, www
.feministing.com/archives/008815.html.

CHAPTER 7

public punishments

1. Claire Luna. "3 Guilty of Sexual Assault in O.C. Gang-Rape Retrial," *Los Angeles Times,*
March 24, 2005.

2. Aya Mueller. "GW sued for negligence, malpractice," *GW Hatchet,* October 4, 2007.

3. Rape, Abuse, & Incest National Network (RAINN).

4. The Happy Feminist. "Maryland's Court Interpretation of Rape Law Is Predicated on the
Notion of Women as Chattel," October 31, 2006, http://happyfeminist.typepad.com.

5. Larry Celona. "Beautiful Co-ed Found Murdered—Body Dumped Near B'klyn High-
way," *New York Post,* February 27, 2006.

6. Veronika Belenkaya and Alison Gendar. "City Beauty Slain by Beast. Tortured & dumped
by road," *New York Daily News,* February 28, 2006.

7. Lauren Elkies. "Slain Student Left Bar Alone After 4 a.m.," *New York Sun,* March 2, 2006;
Donovan Slack. "Fearless in the City. Some Women Still Party as If Invulnerable," *Boston
Globe,* March 9, 2006.

8. NBC News. Transcripts, April 5, 2006.

9. CBS News. Transcripts, March 9, 2006.

10. Jessica Heslam. "WRKO radio host defends talk of victim 'asking for trouble,'" *Boston
Herald,* March 2, 2006.

11. Naomi Schaefer Riley. "Ladies, You Should Know Better," *Wall Street Journal,* April 14,
2006.

12. Katie Roiphe. *The Morning After: Fear, Sex, and Feminism* (New York: Back Bay Books, 1994).

13. Ibid.

14. Melissa McEwan. "Dear Ladies: Please Stop Getting Yourselves Raped," January 3, 2007, *Shakesville,* http://shakespearessister.blogspot.com.

15. Feministing.com. "Joe Francis with yet another sex charge," April 26, 2007, www.feministing.com/archives/006931.html; The Smoking Gun. www.thesmokinggun.com/archive/0419043ggw1.html; Feministing.com. "Girls Gone Wild founder gets community service," December 14, 2006, www.feministing.com/archives/006211.html.

16. Anything & Everything. "'Girls Gone Wild' Cameraman Accused of Raping Minor in Ohio," October 26, 2006, http://ballyblog.wordpress.com.

17. Kieran Crowley. "'Wild' LI Sex Attack—Video Man Busted," *New York Post,* August 7, 2008.

18. Bob Dyer. "Witness says crew was wild before," *Akron Beacon Journal,* October 26, 2006.

19. Claire Hoffman. "'Baby, Give Me a Kiss,'" *Los Angeles Times,* August 6, 2006.

20. Ibid.

21. Deidra J. Fleming. "Out, damned error out, I say!" *Army Lawyer,* May 2005, http://find-articles.com/p/articles/mi_m6052.

22. CBS. "Tables Turned On Alleged Rape Victim," August 28, 2007, www.cbsnews.com.

23. Feministing.com. "ABC News on Duke: The 'Lacrosstitute' Factor," April 17, 2006, www.feministing.com/archives/004868.html; Liz Cox Barrett. "Of Duke, and Princeton, and Jocks, and Sluts," *Columbia Journalism Review,* April 19, 2006, www.cjr.org/behind_the_news/of_duke_and_princeton_and_jock.php.

24. LAist. "OC Cop Gets Off in Court after Masturbating on Stripper During Questionable Traffic Stop," February 10, 2007, www.laist.com.

25. Jill Porter. "Hooker raped and robbed—by justice system?" *Philadelphia Daily News,* October 12, 2007.

26. Feministing.com. "Kos: Getting harassed? Stop blogging." April 12, 2007, www.feministing.com/archives/006858.html.

27. Jill Filipovic. "Hi, I'm Jill, and scummy law school sleazebags have gone after me, too," *Feministe,* March 7, 2007, www.feministe.us/blog/archives/2007.

28. The Pew Research Center for the People & the Press. "A Portrait of 'Generation Next,'" January 9, 2007, http://people-press.org/reports.

29. Heather Mac Donald. "What campus rape crisis?" *Los Angeles Times,* February 24, 2008.

30. Laura Sessions Stepp. "A New Kind of Date Rape," *Cosmopolitan,* www.cosmopolitan.com/sex-love/sex.

31. Ibid.

32. Beth Slovic. "Trial By Facebook," *Willamette Week,* January 9, 2008.

33. Ibid.

34. Dahlia Lithwick. "Gag Order: A Nebraska judge bans the word *rape* from his courtroom," *Slate,* June 20, 2007, www.slate.com/id/2168758.

35. Naomi Schaefer Riley. "Ladies, You Should Know Better," *Wall Street Journal,* April 14, 2006.

CHAPTER 8

beyond manliness

1. Stephen J. Ducat. *The Wimp Factor: Gender Gaps, Holy Wars, and the Politics of Anxious Masculinity* (Boston: Beacon Press, 2004).

2. Ibid., 5.

3. Serano. *Whipping Girl,* 326.

4. CNN. "Arizona criminals find jail too in 'tents,'" July 27, 1999, www.cnn.com/US.

5. Local6.com. "Report: Boy Forced To Wear Skirt As Punishment," February 27, 2004, www.local6.com/money/; *Dartmouth Review.* "Week in Review," May 14, 2001, http://dartreview.com/archives/2001.

6. Melissa Bruen. "My Spring Weekend Nightmare," *Daily Campus,* May 2, 2008.

7. Ibid.

8. Matthew Fitzgerald. "Training Your Girlfriend," *AskMen.com,* www.askmen.com/dating/curtsmith.

9. Peter Rubin. "Is it OK to Demand Anal Sex?" *Details,* July 9, 2007.

10. Ibid.

11. Michael Kimmel. *Guyland: The Perilous World Where Boys Become Men* (New York: HarperCollins, 2008).

12. Ibid., 169–70.

13. Ibid., 219.

14. Scott Jaschik. "Understanding 'Guyland,'" *Inside Higher Ed,* August 21, 2008.

15. James C. Dobson, PhD. "Radical Feminism Shortchanges Boys," Focus on the Family, November 2004, www2.focusonthefamily.com/docstudy.

16. James C. Dobson. *Bringing Up Boys: Practical Advice and Encouragement for Those Shaping the Next Generation of Men* (Carol Stream, IL: Tyndale House, 2001), Chapter 5.

17. *National Review.* "Hail the Male," June 13, 2008.

18. Janice Shaw Crouse. "Feminizing the Nation's Boys," Concerned Women for America, May 21, 2004.

19. Ibid.

20. Harvey C. Mansfield. *Manliness* (New Haven, CT: Yale University Press, 2006).

21. Samuel Jacobs. "Mansfield Calls For 'New Feminism,'" *Harvard Crimson,* October 19, 2005.

22. Ibid.

23. Douglas Rushkoff. "Picture Perfect," in *What Makes a Man: 22 Writers Imagine the Future,* ed. Rebecca Walker (New York: Riverhead Books, 2004).

24. Robert Jensen. "The high cost of manliness," *AlterNet,* September 8, 2006, www.alternet.org/sex/41356.

25. Ibid.

CHAPTER 9
sex, morals, and trusting women

1. Miriam Grossman. *Sense & Sexuality: The College Girl's Guide to Real Protection in a Hooked-Up World* (Herndon, VA: Clare Boothe Luce Policy Institute, 2008), 13.

2. Ibid., 20.

3. Katha Pollitt. "Virginity or Death!," *Nation,* May 12, 2005.

4. Monitoring the Future. Monitoring the Future (1975–2005), www.monitoringthefuture.org.

5. Michael Males. "Have 'Girls Gone Wild'?" in *Beating Up On Girls: Girls, Violence, Demonization and Denial* (New York: New York Press, 2009 (at press)).

6. The National Campaign to Prevent Teen and Unplanned Pregnancy. National pregnancy rates for teens, aged 15–19.

7. J. S. Santelli et al. "Exploring recent declines in adolescent pregnancy in the United States: the contribution of abstinence and increased contraceptive use," *American Journal of Public Health* 97 (2007): 150–56.

8. Advocates for Youth. "Adolescent Protective Behaviors: Abstinence and Contraceptive Use," www.advocatesforyouth.org/publications.

9. Advocates for Youth. "Adolescent Pregnancy and Childbearing in the United States," www.advocatesforyouth.org/publications.

10. Jaclyn Friedman and Jessica Valenti. *Yes Means Yes: Visions of Female Sexual Power and a World Without Rape* (Berkeley, CA: Seal Press, 2009).

11. Ibid., 38.

12. Ibid.

13. Advocates for Youth. "Adolescent Sexual Behavior. I: Demographics," www.advocatesforyouth.org/publications.

14. Levy. *Female Chauvinist Pigs*, 82.

15. Kara Jesella. "Female Chauvinist Pigs," *AlterNet*, October 3, 2005.

16. Jennifer Baumgardner. "Feminism Is a Failure, and Other Myths," *AlterNet*, November 17, 2005, www.alternet.org/rights/28237.

17. Natalie Angier. *Woman: An Intimate Geography* (New York: Random House, 1999), 366.

18. George Lakoff. "Metaphor, Morality, and Politics, Or, Why Conservatives Have Left Liberals in the Dust," *Social Research*, summer 1995.

CHAPTER 10

post-virgin world

1. Technorati. "State of the Blogosphere," 2008, http://technorati.com/blogging/state-of-the-blogosphere.

2. Family and Youth Services Bureau. Discretionary Grant Awards: FY 2008, www.acf.hhs.gov/programs/fysb/content/docs/08_discgrantawards.htm.

3. Medical Institute. Mission statement, www.medinstitute.org.

4. www.takeissuetakecharge.org; www.communityactionkit.org.

5. www.mavaw.org.

6. www.stopviolence.com.

7. www.meetup.com.

8. Right Wing News. "America Has An Obsession With Virginity? And It's Hurting Young Women? Really?" October 6, 2008, www.rightwingnews.com.

9. Network of enlightened Women. "New feminist book: The Purity Myth," October 8, 2008, http://blog.enlightenedwomen.org.

10. House of Eratosthenes. "Best Sentence XLII," October 6, 2008, http://mkfreeberg.webloggin.com/best-sentence-xlii.

11. Cassy Fiano. "Putting out is SO much better for girls than abstinence," October 6, 2008, www.cassyfiano.com.

12. Erika Anderson. "Is Purity a Myth?" http://culture11.com/blogs/lady-blog/2008/10/09/is-purity-a-myth.

13. http://blackandmissing.blogspot.com.

resources

THE FOLLOWING LIST OF RESOURCES CAN
ALSO BE FOUND AT WWW.PURITYMYTH.COM.

organizations

ABORTION ACCESS PROJECT

The Abortion Access Project advocates access to safe abortion for all women in the United States; looks for gaps in abortion access that no one else is addressing, and seeks to create and support innovative responses to these gaps; and works with local partners to achieve locally driven, locally relevant goals, then introduces these projects to national organizations also interested in expanding access. (www.abortionaccess.org)

AMERICAN ASSOCIATION OF UNIVERSITY WOMEN

This national organization promotes women's educational equality. Not only does AAUW do terrific advocacy work, it also provides comprehensive research materials on young women and education. (www.aauw.org)

BLACK WOMEN'S HEALTH IMPERATIVE

The Black Women's Health Imperative is the only organization devoted solely to advancing the health and wellness of America's black women and girls through advocacy, community health and wellness education, and leadership development. (www.blackwomenshealth.org)

CENTER FOR AMERICAN WOMEN AND POLITICS

Housed at Rutgers University in New Jersey, CAWP is the leading source of scholarly research and current data about American women's political participation. (www.cawp.rutgers.edu)

CENTER FOR REPRODUCTIVE RIGHTS

A nonprofit legal-advocacy organization dedicated to promoting and defending women's reproductive rights worldwide. The center works on Capitol Hill and in the courts; its website features information on national legislation affecting women's reproductive health and rights. (www.reproductiverights.org)

CENTER FOR WOMEN POLICY STUDIES

The Center for Women Policy Studies was founded in 1972 as the first feminist-policy analysis and research institution in the United States. Its mission is to shape public policy to improve women's lives and preserve their human rights. (www.centerwomenpolicy.org)

CHOICE USA

This youth-led organization supports emerging leaders in the reproductive-justice movement; it's an amazing resource and group for younger women. (www.choiceusa.org)

FAIR FUND, INC.

FAIR works globally to engage youth, especially young women, in civil society. It heightens awareness of human trafficking and domestic violence, informs young people about sexual-assault prevention, and promotes the development of youth capacity-building programs. (www.fairfund.org)

FAMILY VIOLENCE PREVENTION FUND

This antiviolence organization works both organizationally and in direct service. FVPF also helped to develop the Violence Against Women Act, passed by Congress in 1994. Its website is a good place to look for statistics and resources on intimate-partner violence and rape. (http://endabuse.org)

GIRLS, INC.

This organization for girls and young women promotes self-esteem, confidence, and independence through programs that address math and science education, pregnancy and drug abuse prevention, media literacy, economic literacy, adolescent health, violence prevention, and sports participation. The group and its website are also great resources for people doing research about girls. (www.girlsinc.org)

GUTTMACHER INSTITUTE

The Guttmacher Institute advances sexual and reproductive health worldwide through an interrelated program of social science research, public education, and policy analysis. This is the go-to organization to consult about women's reproductive health. (www.guttmacher.org)

INSTITUTE FOR WOMEN'S POLICY RESEARCH

IWPR researches poverty and welfare, employment and earnings, work and family issues, health and safety, and women's civic and political participation. (www.iwpr.org)

NARAL PRO-CHOICE AMERICA

For more than 30 years, NARAL Pro-Choice America has been the nation's leading advocate for privacy and a woman's right to choose. With more than one million members and supporters, NARAL is fighting to protect the pro-choice values of freedom and privacy. (www.prochoiceamerica.org)

NATIONAL ASIAN PACIFIC AMERICAN WOMEN'S FORUM

NAPAWF is the only national, multi-issue organization dealing with Asian Pacific American women's issues in the United States. The organization's mission is to build a movement to advance social justice and human rights for APA women and girls. (www.napawf.org)

NATIONAL COALITION OF WOMEN AND GIRLS IN EDUCATION

This nonprofit organization is dedicated to improving educational opportunities for girls and women. The group also addresses the implementation of Title IX. (www.ncwge.org)

NATIONAL COALITION AGAINST DOMESTIC VIOLENCE

This national organization working to end violence against women not only lobbies for efforts opposing domestic violence, but also offers financial education programs for women and houses the only direct-service program that offers reconstructive surgery to domestic-violence survivors. (www.ncadv.org)

NATIONAL COUNCIL FOR RESEARCH ON WOMEN

The council comprises a network of more than one hundred U.S. research, advocacy, and policy centers; part of its mission is to ensure "fully informed debate, policies, and practices to build a more inclusive and equitable world for women and girls." (www.ncrw.org)

NATIONAL INDIAN WOMEN'S HEALTH RESOURCE CENTER

NIWHRC is a national nonprofit organization whose mission is to help American Indian and Alaska Native women achieve optimal health and well-being throughout their lives. (www.niwhrc.org)

NATIONAL INSTITUTE FOR REPRODUCTIVE HEALTH

The National Institute for Reproductive Health offers breakthrough education programs and encourages advocacy strategies proven to expand access to quality reproductive healthcare. (www.nirhealth.org)

NATIONAL LATINA INSTITUTE FOR REPRODUCTIVE HEALTH

The mission of NLIRH is to secure the fundamental human right to reproductive health and justice for Latinas, their families, and their communities through public education, community mobilization, and policy advocacy. (www.latinainstitute.org)

NATIONAL NETWORK TO END DOMESTIC VIOLENCE

NNEDV is a membership and advocacy organization of state domestic-violence coalitions; it makes sure that national policymakers hear and understand those coalitions' needs. (www.nnedv.org)

NATIONAL PARTNERSHIP FOR WOMEN & FAMILIES

Formerly the Women's Legal Defense Fund, the National Partnership was founded in 1971 and uses public education and advocacy to push for workplace equality, healthcare, and policies that help people meet work and family demands. (www.nationalpartnership.org)

NATIONAL SEXUAL VIOLENCE RESOURCE CENTER

The center serves as the nation's principal information and resource center regarding all aspects of sexual violence. (www.nsvrc.org)

NATIONAL WOMEN'S POLITICAL CAUCUS

The National Women's Political Caucus is a bipartisan, multicultural grassroots organization dedicated to increasing women's participation in the political field and creating a political power base designed to achieve equality for all women. (www.nwpc.org)

PLANNED PARENTHOOD FEDERATION OF AMERICA

PPFA is the nation's leading women's healthcare provider, educator, and advocate, serving women, men, teens, and families. Planned Parenthood provides quality healthcare and services, offers medically accurate information, and advances effective health policies. (www.plannedparenthood.org)

RAPE, ABUSE & INCEST NATIONAL NETWORK

The Rape, Abuse & Incest National Network is the nation's largest anti-sexual assault organization. RAINN operates the National Sexual Assault Hotline at 1.800.656.HOPE and the National Sexual Assault Online Hotline; publicizes the hotlines' free, confidential services; and educates the public about sexual assault. (www.rainn.org)

SAFE HORIZON

Safe Horizon is the nation's leading victim-assistance organization. Based in NYC, the group provides support, addresses violence, and promotes justice for victims of crime and abuse, their families, and their communities. (www.safehorizon.org)

SISTERSONG WOMEN OF COLOR REPRODUCTIVE HEALTH COLLECTIVE

SisterSong is a network of local, regional, and national grassroots agencies representing women of color in the United States. The collective works to educate women of color and policymakers on reproductive and sexual health and rights, and advocates access to health services, information, and resources that are culturally and linguistically appropriate. (www.sistersong.net)

THE WHITE HOUSE PROJECT

The White House Project aims to advance women's leadership in all communities and sectors—including the U.S. presidency—by filling the leadership pipeline with a richly diverse critical mass of women. (www.thewhitehouseproject.org)

WOMEN'S SPORTS FOUNDATION

The Women's Sports Foundation—the leading authority on women's and girls' participation in athletics—advocates for equality, educates the public, conducts research, and offers grants to endorse sports and physical activity for girls and women. (www.womenssportsfoundation.org)

WOMEN'S VOICES. WOMEN VOTE

Women's Voices. Women Vote started with one goal in mind: to increase unmarried women's participation in the electorate and policymaking process. (www.wvwv.org)

YOUNGER WOMEN'S TASK FORCE

A project of the National Council of Women's Organizations, YWTF is a nationwide, grassroots movement that focuses on issues affecting younger women; it's also an amazing resource for women who want to organize locally. YWTF has youth-led chapters across the country. (www.ywtf.org)

A note about local organizations: The organizations and groups listed here work overwhelmingly at the national level. But I can't stress enough how important finding *local, grassroots groups* in your community is.

magazines

Finding progressive news sources isn't always easy; these magazines are a great place to start.

The American Prospect (www.prospect.org)

Bitch magazine (www.bitchmagazine.com)

ColorLines (www.colorlines.com)

In These Times (www.inthesetimes.com)

make/shift (www.makeshiftmag.com)

Ms. magazine (www.msmagazine.com)

New Moon (www.newmoon.com)

Salon (www.salon.com)

Shameless magazine (www.shamelessmag.com)

The Nation (www.thenation.com)

Tint Magazine (www.tintmag.com)

WireTap (www.wiretapmag.org)

Women's eNews (http://womensenews.org)

Women's Media Center (www.womensmediacenter.com)

blogs

Alas, a Blog (www.amptoons.com/blog)

AngryBlackBitch (http://angryblackbitch.blogspot.com)

AngryBrownButch (www.angrybrownbutch.com)

Bitch Ph.D. (http://bitchphd.blogspot.com)

Black and Missing but not Forgotten (http://blackandmissing.blogspot.com)

Broadsheet (www.salon.com/mwt/broadsheet/index.html)

Change Happens: the SAFER Blog (http://safercampus.org/blog)

Echidne of the Snakes (www.echidneofthesnakes.blogspot.com)

Economic Woman (http://economicwoman.com)

Feminist Law Professors (http://feministlawprofs.law.sc.edu)

Feministe (http://feministe.us/blog)

Finally, a Feminism 101 Blog (http://finallyfeminism101.wordpress.com)

Global Voices Online (www.globalvoicesonline.org)

I Blame the Patriarchy (http://blog.iblamethepatriarchy.com)

Lynne d Johnson (www.lynnedjohnson.com/diary)

Muslimah Media Watch (http://muslimahmediawatch.blogspot.com)

Our Bodies, Our Blog (www.ourbodiesourblog.org)

Pam's HouseBlend (www.pamshouseblend.com)

Pandagon (www.pandagon.net)

PopPolitics (www.poppolitics.com)

Racewire (www.racewire.org)

Racialicious (www.racialicious.com)

Radical Doula (http://radicaldoula.wordpress.com)

RH RealityCheck (www.rhrealitycheck.org)

Shakespeare's Sister (www.shakesville.com)

Shapely Prose (http://kateharding.net)

The Curvature (http://thecurvature.com)

Trans Group Blog (http://transgroupblog.blogspot.com)

WIMN's Voices (www.wimnonline.org/WIMNsVoicesBlog)

Women and Hollywood (http://womenandhollywood.blogspot.com)

Women of Color Blog (http://brownfemipower.com)

Women's Health News (http://womenshealthnews.wordpress.com)

books

How the Pro-Choice Movement Saved America
by Cristina Page

Killing the Black Body: Race, Reproduction, and the Meaning of Liberty
by Dorothy Roberts

Promiscuities: The Secret Struggle for Womanhood
by Naomi Wolf

Rapture Ready!: Adventures in the Parallel Universe of Christian Pop Culture
by Daniel Radosh

Righting Feminism: Conservative Women and American Politics
by Ronnee Schreiber

Sex in Crisis: The New Sexual Revolution and the Future of American Politics
by Dagmar Herzog

The War on Choice: The Right-Wing Attack on Women's Rights and How to Fight Back
by Gloria Feldt

Virgin: The Untouched History
by Hanne Blank

Virginity Lost: An Intimate Portrait of First Sexual Experiences
by Laura Carpenter

index

DePetro, John: 149–150
depression: 53, 55, 186
desirability: commodifying underage 61–62; of naiveté 65; of purity porn stars 91
desire: 199
Details: 173, 174
Dial, Ashley: 43
Dickens, Morgan: 103
Dobson, James: 176
dolls, love: 87
dominance: 173, 174
double standards: in alcohol consumption 164–165; protection/punishment 188–189; of sexual "dirtiness" 41–42; *see also* virgin/whore dichotomy
drinking, as rape risk: 148–149, 163
Drinking Liberally: 211
Ducat, Stephen J.: 168–169
Duplantis, Lloyd: 137
Durham, M. Gigi: 63, 64, 65, 79–80, 207–208

E

Eden, Dawn: 47–48, 55–56, 57
education: comprehensive sex 119, 120; equality in 240; of friends/peers 207–208; sex as "dirty" in 32–34; on violence toward women 208; *see also* abstinence-only education
electron-Blue: 24
emergency contraception (EC): 128–129, 136–137, 219
emotions: 169–170
empowerment: 106, 151, 164, 197
equality, as blamed for rape: 160–161, 164–165, 178, 179
ethics. *See* morality
evangelicals, Christian: 26
Evert, Jason: 34

F

Facebook: 117
Fair Fund, Inc.: 241
fame: 89–90
Family Research Council: 71

family values: 138–139
Family Violence Prevention Fund: 208, 241
fashion: Abercrombie & Fitch boycott 49; infantalizing 72–73; schoolgirl 76
FDA: 128–129
federal funding: for Abstinence Clearinghouse 113; for abstinence education 104, 111–113, 218; for crisis pregnancy centers 206; for purity balls 69, 217; state refusal of 118
Female Chauvinist Pigs (Levy): 90, 197
female genital mutilation: 74
The Female Thing (Kipnis): 42–43
femininity: 167–170
feminism: blogs 205; feminists against abstinence education 118; as feminizing boys 177–178; as harming morality 56–57; porn informed by 86, 210, 210–211; pro-sex 98; vs. raunch culture 196–197; scapegoating 163, 164–165; treatises on rape 146; as used by the virginity movement 37–38; virginity movement against 96–97, 180
Feministing.com: abstinence education discussion on 103; as activism forum 118, 206; anti-choice activists against 137; electron-Blue 24; Friedman, Ann 52; Martin, Courtney 90; reaction to this book on 212
feminization: 170, 178, 179
femiphobia: 168–169, 177
fetal protection laws: 126–127, 140–141
fetishizing women: 28, 96
Figueroa, Lisseth: 74
Filipovic, Jill: 26, 159
Focus on the Family: 26, 35, 67, 81, 176
forgiveness: 203
foster care: 114
Francis, Joe: 152–154
Fredell, Janie: 25
Friedman, Ann: 52, 67
Friedman, Jaclyn: 194
Friends: 92
Full Frontal Feminism (Valenti): 170

pleasure: absent from virginity movement 56; exempt from vaginal rejuvenation 74; as a man's domain 107; separating sex from 43; taboo of 196

Poe, Edgar Allen: 148

politics: of abstinence-only education 118–119; affecting 208–209; of commercial porn 95; conservative, in schools 115; denied to women 143; gender stereotyping in 168; legislating reproductive rights 123–128; paternalistic 139–140; science as serving 54; separation of church and state 112; sex as affecting 55; of virginity fetish 14; virginity movement in 23

Pollitt, Kathy: 189

pop culture: abstinence morality in 26–27; sexualization of 92; virginity trend in 10, 28

The Porning of America (Sarracino and Scott): 82

pornography: 81–99; activism against 91–96; commodifying 81–82; as debasing 86; feminism and 210; modern exaggeration of 83; outside male control 95, 97–98; outside the status quo 93; re-thinking 97; sales statistics 84–85; as skewing "normal" 74; virginal 76

Posey, Julie: 78

poverty: 138, 139, 192

power: 143, 173

pregnancy: coercion 114; criminalizing 140–141, 142; crisis centers 112–113; fetal rights 126–127, 140–141, 219; misinformation on 105; as personal choice 199–200; pro-lifers on 124; requiring ultrasounds for 133–134; and secondary virginity 35–36; socio-economic factors 192; statistics 59, 192

pressure: parental 37; peer 25–26

pro-life movement: 124

The Pro-Life Activist's Encyclopedia: 124

promiscuity: HPV vaccine as prompting 70–71; media reports of 45–46; pathologizing 107; Plan B as prompting 129, 130

prostitution: 77, 156–157

Prude: How the Sex-Obsessed Culture Hurts Young Women (and America, Too!) (Liebau): 47, 55, 56

public sphere harassment: 158, 159

"Pure Fashion" shows: 49

Pure Love (Evert): 34

"Pure Love Promise": 34

purity: as brainless 27; connections with porn 87, 89, 91, 95; fathers' protection of daughters' 66, 69; feminism as lacking 164; vs. hypersexualization 9–10; innate 48–49; legislating 123; as misogynistic myth 10–11, 201; and normalization of rape 147–148, 157; as powerless 142–143; in secondary virginity 34–35; veneration of 28; via virginity 69; women of color as denied 158

purity balls: 10, 31, 32, 65–67, 68, 217

Pussycat Dolls: 97

Q R

queer sexuality: 109, 200

questions for discussion: 221–222

radical feminism: 177–178, 180

rape: date 150; defined by Senator Henry (D-TN) 145; denial of victim's rights 145–146; by Girls Gone Wild crew 152–154; "gray" 160–163; as innate to masculinity 174, 175; legislating 146; omission of term 162–163; proving pregnancy from 138; shaming of victims 108–109; un-rapeability 147, 157; victims as blamed for 147–151, 155; women's equality as blamed for 160–161, 164–165

Rape, Abuse & Incest National Network: 245

raunch culture: 97, 197

raves: 72

Ray, Audacia: 98–99

Real Dolls: 87–89

Real Hot 100: 204

"reality" porn: 85–86

Rees, Katie: 29

Reid, Sergeant Ronald: 146

51; no gray area in 213; and normalization of rape 148; promotion of 82–83

W X Y Z

acknowledgments

Writing this book would have been impossible without the support of many people, but the biggest thanks go to my partner, Andrew Golis—thank you for believing that I can do anything, and for gently stopping me when I try to do everything.

My parents, Phil and Nancy, and my sister, Vanessa, have been a source of constant encouragement and inspiration. You've made everything I do possible, and I'll be forever grateful. I love you all.

Thanks to my friends who continue to surprise and challenge me every day: Gwen Beetham, Ann Friedman, Courtney Martin, Kate Mogulescu, Samhita Mukhopadhyay, and Miriam Perez.

I owe a tremendous debt of gratitude to the readers of Feministing.com.

I may not know you all by name, but knowing that you're there—having amazing conversations in the comments section, blogging, or even just reading quietly at your computers—makes me happy every day. Thank you.

And lastly, thank you to Seal Press—especially to my editor and friend Brooke Warner—for believing in me from the beginning. Your continued support means the world to me.

about the author

© ADAM JOSEPH

Jessica Valenti is the founder and editor of Feministing.com, a popular blog and online community. She is the author of *Full Frontal Feminism: A Young Woman's Guide to Why Feminism Matters* and *He's a Stud, She's a Slut . . . and 49 Other Double Standards Every Woman Should Know,* and coeditor of the anthology *Yes Means Yes: Visions of Female Sexual Power and a World Without Rape.*

Jessica's writing has appeared in *The Nation,* the *Guardian* (U.K.), *Ms.* magazine, and *Bitch* magazine, and on Salon.com and Babble.com. She received her master's degree in women's and gender studies from Rutgers University, where she is now a part-time lecturer. Jessica lives with her partner, Andrew, in Queens, New York.

selected titles from seal press

For more than thirty years, Seal Press has published groundbreaking books. By women. For women. Visit our website at www.sealpress.com. Check out the Seal Press blog at www.sealpress.com/blog.

Yes Means Yes: Visions of Female Sexual Power and A World Without Rape, by Jaclyn Friedman and Jessica Valenti. $15.95, 1-58005-257-6. This powerful and revolutionary anthology offers a paradigm shift from the "No Means No" model, challenging men and women to truly value female sexuality and ultimately end rape.

Full Frontal Feminism: A Young Woman's Guide to Why Feminism Matters, by Jessica Valenti. $15.95, 1-58005-201-0. A sassy and in-your-face look at contemporary feminism for women of all ages.

He's A Stud, She's A Slut and 49 Other Double Standards Every Woman Should Know, by Jessica Valenti. $13.95, 1-58005-245-2. With sass, humor, and aplomb, Full Frontal Feminism author Jessica Valenti takes on the obnoxious double standards women encounter every day.

Feminism and Pop Culture: Seal Studies, by Andi Zeisler. $12.95, 1-58005-237-1. Andi Zeisler, cofounder of Bitch magazine, traces the impact of feminism on pop culture (and vice versa) from the 1940s to today.

Colonize This!: Young Women of Color on Today's Feminism, edited by Daisy Hernandez and Bushra Rehman. $16.95, 1-58005-067-0. An insight into a new generation of brilliant, outspoken women of color—how they are speaking to the concerns of a new feminism, and their place in it.

Body Outlaws: Rewriting the Rules of Beauty and Body Image, edited by Ophira Edut, foreword by Rebecca Walker. $15.95, 1-58005-108-1. Filled with honesty and humor, this groundbreaking anthology offers stories by women who have chosen to ignore, subvert, or redefine the dominant beauty standard in order to feel at home in their bodies.